Stop Crack/Cocaine and reclaim your life

Louise Clarke Bsc (Hons)

Stop using Crack/Cocaine and reclaim your life.

Copyright (c) 2011

ISBN -13:978-1482762303

Stop using crack /cocaine and reclaim your life

Contents

		page number
Preface		4
Chapter 1	Who uses crack?	7
Chapter 2	How long does it take to become addicted	9
Chapter 3	Am I addicted	14
Chapter 4	Lovely food and weather	16
Chapter 5	What are the medical risks?	25
Chapter 6	How am I training (will un-train) myself in addiction	32
Chapter 7	Why get off	39
Chapter 8	How to use and stay in control	41
Chapter 9	Men and Women are different	43
Chapter 10	Seven types of users	48

Chapter 11   Dealing with cravings both physical   53
              and mental.

Chapter 12   Mental cravings -mind games mental Tia chi   63
              against cravings

Chapter 13   How to stop sensory/physical cravings   66

Chapter 14   Dealing with depression, boredom and   69
              other factors involved in stopping

Chapter 15   How am I going to get off and stay off?   76

Chapter 16   Different strokes for different folks   87

Chapter 17   What about pregnancy   94

Chapter 18   Disease model addressed (who gets hooked)   96

Chapter 19   What about heroin, methadone, weed   99
              and alcohol

Chapter 20   Spiritual tools   100

Glossary   102

Reading list   104

Who is Louise Clarke? 106

Chapter 1 'It's here' 107

Chapter 2 Becoming a drug counsellor 113

Chapter 3 I outgrew my pot, & didn't need pruning 120

Chapter 4 Constructive dismissal 124

Chapter 5 I found a way – free at last 127

Poems

A poem I was inspired to write 95 131

No thank you crack man 133

Preface

I decided to write this book 13 years ago, I had been working with crack users for 7 years and had made it my business to learn all there was to learn.
When I first began (1991) I had just finished my degree in psychology and was attending a counselling course. A requirement of that course was that I did some voluntary work, I approached a drugs service and they welcomed me to work for them. Not long there a women came in saying 'I'm a crack head someone better see me now!' Crack users were not coming to drug projects at this time and projects weren't inviting them; they didn't know how to help them. As she came in, all my colleges disappeared. I told her I don't know anything about crack but I would try to help her. This I did and on the back of that many of her mates followed demanding to see me. My boss said I had something special and employed me to work specifically with this client group.

When I began there wasn't much information available on crack in this country, and no internet. I managed to obtain some books from the states but they only talked about what the drug was and how it worked biologically. Not how to help people get off.

After working with them trying my best to understand their experience, problems in stopping etc, it became apparent that there were 6 types of users. And very few tools to help them. Recovery patterns emerged and familiar tricks were shown by crack like the drug had a personality.
I stayed in the voluntary sector until 1997, but the politics

changed here in England, on the way the services run. Previously government provided very little funding to drug services and virtually none for crack users. Thus services received mainly charitable funds. And because no one was really tackling crack users I was allowed to develop a service to meet the client's needs.

Government funding later increased for drug services, but in return they wanted more information on the clients, to show what public monies was being used for. Although understandable this meant I would need to ask intrusive questions on first appointment; and for many clients paranoia is present thus this need to ask questions can get in the way. I therefore decided to set up my own private and independent service; 1997 which I funded by providing training to professionals working with crack users throughout Britain.

Through working with all types of users I come to realise there are basically 6 types of users. I was in the process of writing this book when along came a client who didn't fit. Didn't make much sense she behaved like a 24/7 user yet had stopped using. This type 7 I came to learn involved other elements that involves issues that sit outside the BOX of general public thinking. I am still trying to grasp the whole picture 12 years in.

In this book I try to help you the users understand the drug better,

Knowledge is power. I want to give you the tools to reduce the cravings and stay clean. I explain the recovery process stage by stage so you will know what to expect. With the knowledge, the tools and a realistic view of the situation there is no reason why you can't stop using.

There are myths out there that you can't get off crack, maybe you think you are too bad on it, too weak, but the truth is you can reclaim your life, it belongs to you not crack. I have never seen one client who wants to stop and can't. You can and you will.

Best wishes for your success

Louise Clarke

Show the world who you were meant to be!

I would like to give thanks here to all those that have helped me along this road of learning; encouraging and supporting me and proof reading this book. Believing this book could happen.

That is –
Nazlyn, Veronica, Delrose, Ann, Leticia, Isaac, Marg, Zena, Ashley, David, Ju
And all the clients I have ever had the privileged to learn from. Thank you!!!!!

I also would like to give thanks to the Lord for guiding me safely along the journey I needed to take to gain this knowledge and understanding. Giving me the courage to believe anything is possible and staying fearless no matter what. Providing me with the experience of seeing miracle after miracle unfold. May this book be blessed and reach all those in need.

Chapter 1   Who uses Crack?

Firstly I would say no specific group of people use Crack/cocaine it's an equal opportunities drug, available to all. It doesn't discriminate. Even the price is adjusted to meet the needs of your spending power.

Wealthy people can still pay huge amounts to purchase a gram of coke or lump of coke (crack). Poor people can have it at reduced price, even free sometimes to start you off. The media has done its best to create an illusion that crack is for Black people and that coke is for rich people, by only delivering stories that fit these profiles, but because it is an equal ops drug, all types of people have the opportunity to try.

Players and plodders

Saying that, I do think crack /cocaine attracts a certain type of person, it attracts players and potentially major players and reduces them to plodders. The potential players may feel they are someone special but are not getting the openings in life, when they take crack/cocaine they feel they are players already. Players can be impatient people and crack/cocaine gives you a feeling of instant success, to begin with, then it aims to remove every chance you had. You may already be successful in your life, but crack will in time destroy your success. Openings come but you blow them, thanks to a little help from crack to make sure you mess up the chance. When you take on this realisation you can see what sort of function crack/cocaine serves to keep the under classes on the bottom;

for by removing the potential players who is going to lead the way for change?!!!

Chapter 2 How long does it take to become addicted

Grow your own

The process of the relationship with crack is such; it is like you're planting a seed in your brain the first time you use it. But seeds don't just sprout over night, you have to water them. They go through an incubation period and in time after regular watering a little shoot comes through. With crack if you water the seed regular in 6-7 months your shoot will come through. And you'll know when it has happened because you start dreaming about it, can't stop thinking about it. Up until it sprouts you may use loads more than you intended, but it isn't addiction: you could stop! But after 6 months it's a different ball game, you can't stop yourself even starting.

The picture is like so:

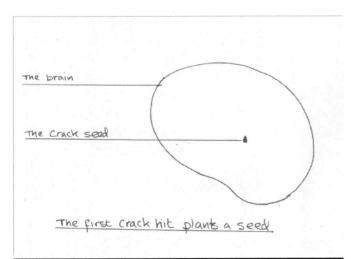

The brain

The Crack seed

The first crack hit plants a seed

Diagram 1: planting seed
The brain with a crack seed, first hit you plant the seed

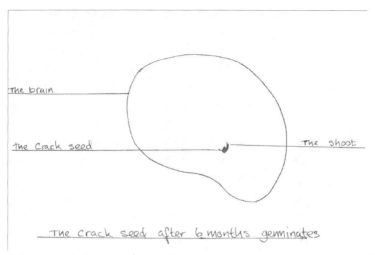

The brain

the Crack seed

The shoot

The crack seed after 6 months germinates

Diagram 2   after 6 months a seed shoots, addiction starts

Germination occurs normally around 6/7 months, here cravings become compulsive.

Keep watering it and soon it will become a strong tree.

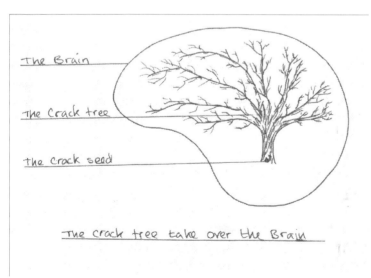

The Brain

The Crack tree

the crack seed

The crack tree take over the Brain

Diagram 3: Tree takes over

Meanwhile the tree suffocates the positive you, telling you what to do. Asking you to do things you wouldn't normally do. You feel your will to fight for full control over your life is shrinking. Consequently you don't feel good about yourself. Which weakens your fight further, leaving you with thoughts of what's the point if I fail?

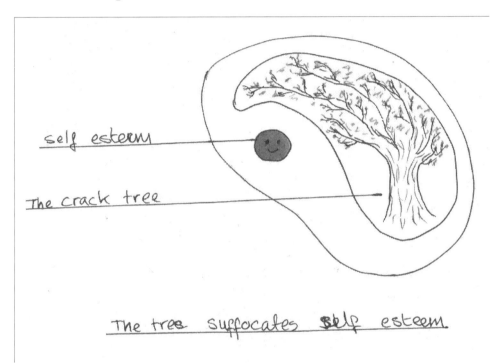

self esteem

The crack tree

The tree suffocates self esteem.

Diagram 4: self/crack

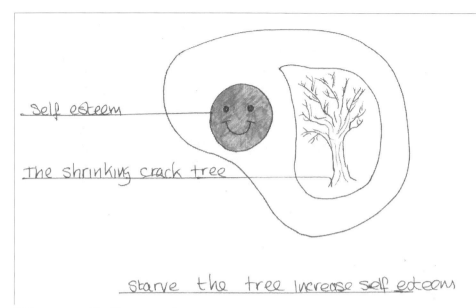

Self esteem

The shrinking crack tree

Starve the tree increase self esteem

Diagram 5: Starve the tree

In order to get yourself back into a position of control you need to stop watering the tree to be freed from its suffocation. A tree needs water to survive, without it, it dies. If you stop watering the tree in your brain with crack then it will gradually shrivel up and die. Meanwhile your old self comes back and you start growing again.

Within a month the tree will lose its leaves, pass 2 years and it will be a seed again. You cannot remove the seed. But like in Africa once you water the dried up soil the seeds sprout again. The struggle you foresee in stopping may put you off trying. The struggle is not the same for the whole 2 years it takes to get rid of the tree. The first month getting rid of the leaves is the hardest part (craving wise). There are different stages of recovery you will go through.

You may find stopping completely too difficult, in that case try to reduce how often you use: this will at least weaken the tree. When it comes to getting from cutting down to abstinence you will need to focus on the task and use the tools that will assist you in your fight.

Chapter 3   Am I addicted?

Crack isn't all it's cracked up to be

So you use crack!   Maybe you don't think you have a problem, maybe you recognise you do. Maybe you're not sure. There's a very simple way of finding out. If you use daily you probably won't need to do this test as you will probably be aware it is a problem, but if you use fortnightly you may be conning yourself that it isn't a problem. 'Why you don't use every day and you don't get sick'. The picture painted of an addict by society is that an addict has to use every day or they will get sick. The truth is addiction is not just this: addiction is when something becomes compulsive. You may say I don't do it because it's compulsive, I do it because I enjoy it; but if your honest with yourself , you know you think about using a lot , you work hard to finance it, and it is not cheap. And when I say work hard I mean work hard.

Simple test

If you still think it is not a problem then do this simple test. Firstly think how often you use. Let's say it is once a month on pay day. 4 weeks, try and do 5 weeks. If you do last 5 weeks you have nothing to worry about yet, but if you've been using for 6 months the chances are you won't be able to do it.

If you think you have a problem or think you may fail the above test, read on. If you don't think you will fail the test you could read out of curiosity or wait until you have your test results.

Love story

You're in love your in love with crack. Crack is like a lover that is no good for you, but you can't leave them. Crack is very manipulative. It will get you to do things you normally wouldn't. It is very cunning it makes you feel powerful and in control, whilst it manipulates the running's of your life. You may keep trying to leave it but you always go back. It suffocates your self esteem. So you stay enslaved. Following cracks agenda. Your own agenda goes out the window.

Chapter 4: Lovely food and weather

There are 2 parts of the brain very important in understanding addiction to Crack.

The first is like a light bulb has been switched on, the more the area is stimulated the brighter it gets and it controls alertness and awareness. In reverse un-stimulated you become tired bored asleep. If damaged you would be comatose.
It is a very old part of the brain, thus works more with instinct than involving much thinking.
It is called the **Reticular formation**.

Another aspect of this part is more subtle. An example would be hearing someone say your name at a party, you hear it, but other people don't. It's something only you are tuned into. Another example is a matter hears her baby crying, whilst others don't hear.

When you smoke crack it first stimulates this area. Making you very awake, alert and like someone turned your lights on in your head. Everything is noticeable you become aware of much more in your surroundings and consequently many of the things in your surroundings become subtly associated with using. The result is at a later date when you see the things in your surroundings that were seen in a high state, you have a high chance of these objects working like triggers to start cravings, and subtle they are. When cocaine (or crack that now in the body is recognised as cocaine) hit's the brain, its first port of call is the **reticular formation.** Here it experiences it like someone has turned all the lights on; no wonder you can't get to sleep. After the lights are all on, it sends a message to the part of the brain that controls our needs/drives called the **Hypothalamus.**

The **Hypothalamus** governs all our drives, that is the drive to eat, drink and have sex, it also tells us when to stop wanting these things: when we have had enough.

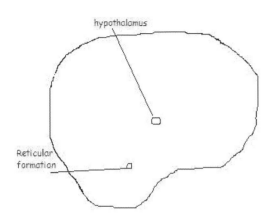

hypothalamus

Reticular
formation

The Brain

Due to cocaine's stimulation of this area it isn't long before cocaine adds itself to the "needs" list. It becomes a need in its self.

With the other needs they are natural, the hypothalamus has sections for both to start and stop, and each need can say "I don't need any more, I've had enough". But nature didn't anticipate the arrival of crack. So crack pushes its self into a position of a nagging need, but there is no creation of a part that signals I've had enough, no stop. In fact the drive to get crack/cocaine overrides all the other need signals. When rats (in labs) become addicted to cocaine they will choose cocaine over all other needs every time and given access to unlimited supply, they will choose to use it to the point of death! There is no stop or I've had enough.

This may help you understand why this drug is so addictive.

The motor way network

Nerves are like a motor way network going all over the body. Passing messages along their networks to and from the brain.

A simple nerve looks like this.

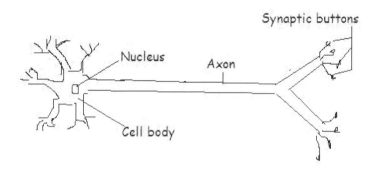

A Simple Nerve cell

The message is received by the **cell body**.
If the stimulation is enough the message will go along the **axon** on to the **pre synaptic button.**

If we enlarge the synapse button even more it would look like this.

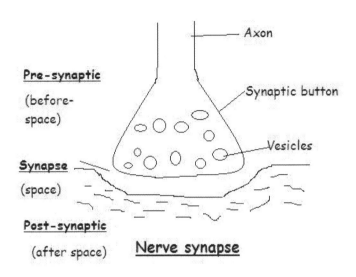

Nerve synapse

Synaptic buttons

In the buttons are little sacks called **Vesicles** that contain different chemicals, technically known as neuro Chemicals.

Don't get scared off by these new words, this info helps you understand and I will make it as simple as can be. All other books on crack use these words and scare people off, once you understand my simple translations those books will be easy for you to read. So read on it will be worth it. !

There are many **neuro chemicals** in the brain, at least 50: all carrying different messages.

I'm only focusing on the main 2.

Pleasure

First **Dopamine**, this is the **chemical of pleasure**, to experience pleasure we need Dopamine, when we experience pleasure Dopamine is released

No Dopamine = no pleasure!

Safety nets
Secondly **Norepinephrine** which is a chemical that is there to stop us getting depressed it's like having rubber rings, it keeps you afloat, stops you from going under.

No Norepinephrine = we sink!

Remember the nerve is stimulated; this causes the release of the chemicals. The chemicals pass across a space to the next nerve again stimulating more chemical release.

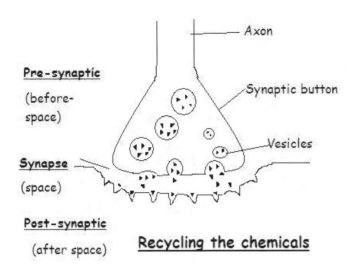

Pre-synaptic

(before-space)

Synapse

(space)

Post-synaptic

(after space)

Recycling the chemicals

Synaptic exchange

Normally after enough stimulation has occurred and the Dopamine has been received into the post synaptic button, the message is passed along that nerve in the same manner, informing the brain of the experience of pleasure. The Dopamine now after completing its task returns back to its previous pre-synaptic button. To be released again at a later date. It gets recycled again and again.

It is **here where things go terribly wrong** when you use crack/cocaine. The release of large amounts Dopamine has occurred, basically nearly all the brain has, hence the high. After being received by the post synaptic button it is sent back, but the **cocaine has changed Dopamine's chemical structure**, it's like the molecules are now wearing silver jackets and the bouncers at the pre-synaptic button door says "we don't recognise you in that jacket, so you can't come back in". The chemical has changed its form through mixing with cocaine and consequently there is no return occurs. That is the dopamine can't get back, so it just floats around giving you a headache. No one is going home.

"oh who cares", you may say when all the dopamine is kicking in, but once the launch has reached its heights and you're plummeting down faster than the speed of light, you first come to find out about the rubber rings I talked of earlier, remember **the Norepinephrine rubber rings that stop you going under and feeling depressed,** whilst you were using all the dopamine, you also threw out all your rubber rings. There has been a total clearance of both chemicals, boy do you feel low!!!!!! Where you may use 3 bits of dopamine to find a joke funny, which also later returns home. When you use **crack all the dopamine is used** and the **Norepinephrine** and **neither are allowed back home**. This explains to you why the highs are so high but now you're on the way down with no rubber rings in sight and it don't feel good as you crash land at the bottom.
Now things can only get worse, no dopamine no pleasure without dopamine we can't even make a smile on our face, the chemical is needed to make the jaw do its thing.

The next part of behaviour is where crack smoking becomes illogical. You think I need more crack to get me out of this pit, plus get back up where I was. You smoke more but you can't get back up there, in fact you are hardly getting out of the ditch on your second journey. This little lift you may experience is the dredges of Dopamine being wiped out from the inside of the pre – synaptic button. And that's your lot, their isn't anymore and there still isn't any sign of the rubber rings. So down you go, you try more rocks to get out of the ditch but it just gets worse. Truth is you can only really get the hit off the first pipe and then the funs over for those who felt it was fun not all do. But you can't stop even if you're aware of this, because remember the hypothalamus earlier, who made crack its greatest need, greater than food, drink, sex well when you use your first pipe of the day, it stimulates the hypothalamus to drive you to use more, so even when you know it's over (the fun bit) you still are compelled to use more.

In addition to this the brain tries always to create balance in the chemistry of the body. It sees there is an imbalance of dopamine being released and reacts by making the receptors, in the post synaptic button to become less sensitive to cope with so much being released. The result of this is when in normal life you try to be happy it will take a lot more!!!

Looking at it the other way round though , when you stop the brain will try to compensate for the lack of dopamine and the small release , and so when it notices the flooding of the chemical has stopped it will produce more receptors to balance things.

You are asking now if you used up all your dopamine and it can't go back then does the brain make more?

Yes it does but normally it only makes a little, slowly. As it is recycled in the normal drug free life. So the production is a slow process I don't know exactly how long the cycle usually takes but people seem to stabilise emotionally after about one month clean.

In a normal situation like a joke being told, there is

stimulation to release the dopamine so we can experience pleasure.

If you do read other books on crack, they may use the word neuro transmitter which means the same as neuro chemicals.

Neuro = nerves

You may be asking what this has got to do with lovely food and weather. Nothing, but if I had written the brain in the title you wouldn't of maybe read this chapter. Well done. I hope it makes sense of how the drug works.

<u>Chapter 5 What are the medical risks?</u>

When we look at crack or cocaine to a certain extent once they enter the body they are the same. Crack on entering the body is registered as being cocaine, Crack is only cocaine and bicarbonate soda mixed together to make it burn longer, the bicarb does nothing in itself.

Now when we look at cocaine a common problem snorters experience is nose bleeds and even sometimes holes in their noses. We need to understand another aspect of the drug. Around 100 years ago coke was used as an anaesthetic for surgical operations. The reason it was used was because it has the ability to restrict blood vessels, thus when doing surgery it reduced the blood loss. Meanwhile it numbed the area, reducing the pain felt.

When coke is snorted into the nose it restricts the blood flow therein .This reduces the blood flow and we all were told by our Mums that if we keep the rubber band too tight round our finger we stop the blood flow: oxygen and nutrition can't flow to the fingertips. Left too long the fingertip would start to rot. This is what happens to constant users noses. Restricted blood flow stops nutrition getting to contact area and therefore starts to rot. Hence the hole where the tissue inside the nose has rotted. This is true for where ever you place the coke constantly on/in your body.

With crack the smoke goes through the mouth down the throat and into the lungs restricting blood flow all along the way. When some crack users lungs are x-rayed you can see scarred tissues and if you use you have probably coughed up black phlegm which is dried blood.

What are the medical risks I am taking?

7 ways to die choose one!

When you look how crack cocaine affects the body, firstly you see it is a stimulant. It stimulates you, wakes you up.

The body has **2 nervous systems**

One is the **central nervous system** made up of the brain and the spinal cord; I have written how crack affects the brain in chapter 4
The second nervous system is the **autonomic system** that without us even thinking our body creates the best bodily rhythms to meet our needs at any given time. Heart rate breathing rate etc

You may of heard of fight or flight reactions , what this is when a threatening situation occurs our body gets ready for action, stimulants induce the release of adrenalin that speeding up the heart rate, breathing, which increases blood flow to muscles to enable us to move fast. It also heats up our body, everything is ordered to go fast.

Crack cocaine is a stimulant meaning it **stimulates the autonomic nervous** system to be sympathetic to our needs, increasing the tempo of the body rhythms.

This is the opposite the drug reaction caused by **heroin, hash, tranquilizers** and **alcohol**. These drugs **slow everything down**. A medical term you may know, these drugs as **depressants**. They depress the body rhythms to slow down and rest.

Now what's all this got to do with medical issues you may say? The fact is if you use too much crack/cocaine or don't stop when your body is screaming at you for a rest, you are heading for an over dose.

7 ways to die

1,First way to die Heart Attack

That is the heart may race so fast, that through the extreme racing caused by crack you have a heart attack. You have probably already experienced heart palpitations, where you can feel your heart pounding in your chest. The heart either goes too fast resulting in a heart attack or it starts losing its rhythm as it is going too fast and again a heart attack.

2, The second way to die is lung failure,

Basically the drug s causing the breathing to increase to such an extent whilst the crack/cocaine is causing the areas of the lungs for absorbing oxygen to restrict, reducing oxygen intake. The lungs struggle to breathe faster, until they get tired and slow right down and eventually stop. = respiratory failure.

3 Third way to die Stroke

Stroke (cerebral haemorrhaging) all this increased heart rate. Increased breathing causes the blood pressure to rise. When blood pressure rises too high it puts a strain on the blood vessels in the brain and if there is a weak vessel it will burst and blood will leak into the brain. Medically known as cerebral (brain) haemorrhaging. This is also known as a stroke and wherever the leakage occurs, damage to that site in the brain may be the result.

4 Forth way to die Epilepsy

Whether you suffer from epilepsy or not crack /cocaine affects the part of the brain responsible for epilepsy (in the limbic system) it gradually weakens the area until fits begin to occur. If you already have epilepsy it will make it worse and this weakness that occurs cannot be reversed. The worst type of seizure is a Grand Mal: this one can take you out.
You may not be aware that you even have fits, if you use on your own. The way you can tell is if when you smoke/use you find you are passing out and don't remember anything when you come round, you have probably been fitting. You may find you have bitten your tongue it may be bleeding.

5 Fifth way to die Blood and sugar levels

If you are diabetic you need to be aware that crack cocaine raises your blood sugar level.

6 Sixth way to die Deficiency in Pseudo-cholinesterase

There is an enzyme in our body that breaks down the cocaine, some people (but this is rare) are deficient in this enzyme and consequently can't break cocaine down. This can be fatal.

7 Seventh way to die Suicide

Sometimes because of the severe lows experienced after using and the added depression, guilt, paranoia shame etc users attempt suicide. Although saying that most crack users solution is to find more crack, I say this as far too often I hear of crack users found dead are reported as suicides when often that isn't the truth but a easy way to solve case.

Deficiency in Vitamins C and B

If you did biology at school you know that vitamin C is for your skin without it we get scurvy. Even cigarettes smoke destroys vitamin C. If you use you probably have noticed your skin is very dry. Vitamin B is for your nervous system. This is self explanatory. When you read all this chapter you see the nervous system is being g knocked for six.

Calcium

As of yet I haven't been able to find any research on how crack/cocaine affects calcium use, but throughout my time working with crack/cocaine users I have seen arthritis in many young people. Why? I don't yet know but I do know calcium is needed to make healthy bones and teeth and while we are on the subject crack/cocaine users teeth become transparent in colour grey and loose. Again no research but reported to me by clients.

Sickle cell/Thalassaemia anaemia

Again I can't obtain any research on sickle cell and crack/cocaine but logically if sickle cell/Thalassaemia is where the blood cells which carry oxygen are sickle shaped rather than round.

And the problem of pain is due to lack of oxygen carried in the blood, it remains logical to conclude that crack reduces oxygen intake in the lungs by restricting the air sacs. Then added reduced oxygen intake must negatively affect sickle cell /Thalassaemia sufferers.

HIV and Aids

Crack will weaken your immune system which HIV effects.

Crack induced psychosis

If you use a lot of crack it can bring about a form of psychosis: visual and auditory hallucinations. That is seeing and hearing things that are not there. You may feel you are mentally ill, you may be diagnosed as mentally ill and in a sense you are, temporarily. There is a **difference** though between **normal psychosis**; where people see and hear hallucinations. And **crack induced psychosis**; the difference is that with **crack induced psychosis you are aware** that you are hallucinating, you question what you see/hear is true.

Crack induced psychosis is caused by chemical overload in the brain, give your brain a rest and it will sort itself out, rebalance. If psychosis does occur ideally stop using. Acupuncture will help greatly in encouraging the brain to rebalance. If you stop using the hallucinations should be gone within 6 weeks. If there do not I recommend you seek psychiatric help. You can ask for help before this although I know a lot of people are reluctant to, it is not necessary unless you feel you are a danger to yourself or others e.g. you may hear voices telling you to do something dangerous or harm another. Sometimes though the hallucinations are not life threatening e.g., you see a bee that isn't really there or snakes climbing you legs.

Reduce the harm you do whilst using

Crack is washed with different things to make it solid and smokable, what it is washed with is important to your health. If it looks white in colour it has most probably been washed with baking soda /bicarbonate soda. But if it is yellowy in colour it has most likely been washed with ammonia, which is a cleaning agent my mum used to clean the drains with. This is very harsh therefore on your throat, avoid it.

What you use to smoke with matters.

Try to avoid using cans to smoke with as the paint on the can is toxic; also the smoke is harsh on your throat. Do not share pipes with others as HEP C and other viruses can be passed on in saliva, also many users have sores around there mouths which increases the risk of passing on HIV.

<u>Chapter 6 How am I training (will untrain) myself in a addiction</u>

This is a very hard chapter to write as it involves a way to enlighten you to the basic mechanisms of natural ways learning occurs; without thought even taking place. It is basic stimulus response training; an area studied extensively in psychology. Behaviour can be manipulated by these mechanisms involved in animal and human learning.

Governed by simple reward and punishment. If a behaviour is rewarded it will increase the chances of the same behaviour occurring again. If on the other hand it receives a punishment it lessens the chances. This is called in psychology **Conditioning.**

Crack ticks all the boxes in conditioning and contains the most efficient principles a psychologist could design. The most effective means of destroying someone of the highest potential, fast.

Understanding the rules of conditioning and how addiction to Crack creates the best conditions to manipulate a person. Conditioning so strong that a habit will be guaranteed to become an addiction; with a compulsive behaviour working at a deep sub- conscious level. Not even necessarily in your awareness. By becoming aware of what you're messing with and how it manipulates you. But you can through understanding use the knowledge and principles against themselves and reclaim your life back. You were meant to be somebody, not a slave to crack. So let me explain these principles further to help you have clarity. To enable you to see what's going on.

Operant conditioning broken down

Operant conditioning is brought about via a reward or punishment set up that encourages or discourages behaviour, where an action /operation is necessary; thus the term operant conditioning.
An action /operation is necessary to get a response or avoid a negative experience.

Positive reinforcement

In simple animal experiments a rat may be required to press a bar (operation) to get a food (reward). Once the rat learns this brings a reward he will be considered to be conditioned to press the bar for food.
With regards to crack, smoking it is the operation /action and it is followed by the high the reward.
The euphoria experienced after smoking crack serves as a positive reinforcer. It increases the chances of the action being repeated again as it comes before the high, the reinforcement.

The quicker the experience of a reward the faster the conditioning occurs. Crack takes 6-7 seconds to reach the brain after inhaling the smoke. This is a very fast reinforcer of behaviour.

In animal experiments it has been shown that rats given a choice will always choose cocaine over food, even females on heat. They will keep pressing the bar choosing cocaine over everything on offer to the point of death.

With crack users they have also been found to choose crack despite punishment like jail, heart attacks, and psychosis and gun shots. They sometimes refuse to stop even when struggling to breath, during lung failure.

The negative consequences of smoking crack are delayed and for punishment to work it has to be instant.

Negative reinforcement

A negative reinforcement is where you do an action to avoid a negative experience.

With our little rat he may press the bar to avoid an electric shock being administered

He is doing the action to avoid the negative experience.

Crack users smoke more crack (action) to avoid the come down crash from using.

The crash is the negative reinforcer it is seen as something to do to avoid crashing by the action of smoking some more.

This reinforces behaviour to not only seek crack for positive reinforcement but also reinforces behaviour to avoid feelings of crash or any discomfort e.g. cravings, anger, depression.

This conditioning is worsened by the fact that the brain in an attempt to address the high levels of neuro chemicals it is experiencing starts to reduce the numbers of receptors in the brain to receive chemicals, like dopamine, in attempt to create balance of the chemistry in the brain. This results in tolerance.

Rewarding only sometimes also works to strengthen conditioning.

This conditioning is then coupled with classical conditioning.

Classical conditioning

Classical conditioning. Here something is repeatedly paired with something you like or dislike, a reward or a punishment is given. Soon the something associated with the reward is learnt to be connected, therefore becomes an indicator that the reward or punishment is coming; a neutral stimuli is coupled with a reward/punishment.

A simple example of this is if we ring a bell every time we give a dog food (reward) so the dog will salivate on hearing the bell. Even if he can't see the food. He has become classically conditioned to the bell. He has developed a conditioned response. The bell is working as a positive reinforcer, it can also work the other way round; by pairing a negative experience a punishment with something.

Neutral stimuli when paired with food (reward) become triggers that bring the physiological response, preparing the body for the reward.

With crack when it is smoked the brain will look for aspects of the situation that it can pair with the experience, to enable it to know when to expect it again.

In addition the first place in the brain crack hits is the reticular formation, a very old part of the brain, which governs awareness. Crack stimulates this area resulting in hyper alert. Consequently the pairing associations that take place whilst using are endless as brain highly alert at the time.

Repeated pairings e.g. crack dealers, pay day, sight of a user, coke can etc will result in each paired association becoming a trigger in their own right. Triggering a physical response in the body as though it was just about to use. Causing cravings everywhere you turn.

So you see crack use is governed by both forms of conditioning that governs behaviour and in the most efficient patterns, demonstrating to you why it is so addictive.

Undoing the conditioning

To undo the conditioning you need to desensitise the brain to the once neutral stimuli. By not reacting to paired stimuli and using. E.g. seeing money and crave but not use. Through not rewarding the cravings you will dilute the connections the brain has previously made and new expectations will be made, for the brain will conclude the old associations are incorrect. Behaviours are not fixed but strongly conditioned to expect use to occur. Therefore you have to un-condition them in a sense.

A way to handle the classically conditioned triggers is to write down a list of things that trigger you to use.

This list will contain things that can and can't be avoided. Those that you can do so! Those that you can't you will need to desensitise yourself to them.

This is done each time you come across them and don't use. Acknowledge the cravings as that, cravings caused by associations the brain has made. By repeated experience of having triggers and not using the brain will desensitise the association.

Do not go testing yourself with triggers, often I have seen clients get clean then go showing off to other users that they can sit with them and not use. This is an ego trip/trick and will end up having you use in time.

It is a good idea to write a list of all your triggers/cues then avoid as many as possible. Those you can't avoid ask for support where you can. For example on money day have non-using person with you, let them hold the money for you as even touching money can bring on cravings. This won't be necessary for ever just first few weeks of stopping.
Avoid people and places associated with crack, even if means you have to walk the long way round to get somewhere.

There will be things you can avoid easy like throwing pipes away, not go near your dealer. Things you can't avoid easy like lighters and money.

Then things you must avoid at all costs, like not going near users or drug.

There may be things you think of later when you come across them, like getting angry. Emotions /behaviours in the past that have been rewarded by using and avoided by using. Like you may be semi-conscious, be somewhat aware that you have rows with people to justify storming off to use.

Add to the list things that come to your attention. Get rid of everything you can that is associated with using.

Start creating positive behaviours that you can do; like sleeping, eating good food, visiting non-using friends.

Avoid uncomfortable feelings they need to be addressed. If you have uncomfortable feelings compelling you to use. (negative reinforcement) you need to find another way to deal with the negative feelings, e.g. depression and boredom and cravings. You need to do the things you enjoy doing. And start to condition yourself to do them when you experience negative emotions. For example if you anger punch a bag. Go to the gym, do some press ups.

if depressed do something you enjoy, Again it is a good idea to write a list of things you enjoy doing ,for when you feel depressed you may not be able to remember.

There are other things to reduce cravings although more complex, so I will go into more detail in later chapters.

Come on stop being a robot, wake up and take control.

Chapter 7 Why get off

Because before you started on this rollercoaster you were destined to be some one that I am sure of. It seems all of you were good at something once and some of you were more than good, you can have it all back if you stop.

I have worked with all types of drug users and you are my favourite type for many reasons: - Firstly you work very hard to get on with life, doing things fast and therefore improving rapidly. Secondly you assert yourselves and get what you need, focused all the way. Thirdly you have fast thinking brains partly due to the crack use altering your approach to life; which used positively can outwit any obstacle.

When you continue using crack these characteristics create a mess for you, making you unfocused with poor concentration and judgment. Stay on the ride and you tell me where the last stop is!!!

If you get off now, before long you will be over the worst and on the road to bigger and better things. If you need support find it.

Your health can regain fast: - sleep, food, drink and skin cream can bring rapid result.

Your concentration will build:-through practice

Your depression will lift

Stop using Crack/Cocaine and reclaim your life.

Your self esteem will increase

Your plans for the future will become a reality

Your life will be yours!!

Come on show yourself and the world what you are capable of

Come out of the dark and into the light

Chapter 8 How to use and stay in control of crack/cocaine

Stop using Crack/Cocaine and reclaim your life.

Chapter 9   Men and Women are different

Men and Women are different in how they relate to the drug, and the drug relates different to them.

Addiction for men ego trouble

This part of the book is difficult for me to write for I believe and have experienced it to be true, but sometimes people don't want to face the truth and in defence they find it easier to condemn me saying I'm wrong. I suppose I need to accept this is your choice. If I don't say what I believe to be true I am guilty of withholding vital information that I have found very useful in enabling men to break free of their addiction to crack, but in saying it and printing it I open myself to all sorts of criticism (I believe to be in defence of the truth). Therefore I brave myself to say it and be done with.

When we look at differences between men and women in how they relate to crack, men's egos tend to become very much involved/entangled and consequently support and maintained their addiction.

1, The first aspect is initially created when men first start using crack. The drug itself brings to men a feeling of power and control. For men this is something they expect to feel in life and when the drug offers that experience: hey presto if they weren't feeling it before - they are hooked.

2, The second aspect is that for many men whether they look good or not, the affects of using crack often leaves them with a feeling like they are super-don, they feel like they are god's gift , often they will be checking themselves in the mirror, to confirm to themselves they are The Man.

3, Coupled with this (if they are using around other users) they will experience women charming them to get them to share their crack, and consequently their view of themselves as 'The Man' is confirmed.
This can escalate even further, if they enter the world of looking to fulfil their sexual fantasies. Because the power of having some crack or money to share with other women crack users, will often result in him being able.
To fulfil his fantasies (for a lick on his pipe), what power what control.
I must point out here though that not all men go along this path, nor do all women crack users offer to fulfil fantasies for crack , but if a man wants it , there are places he can find it, and some women users will provide it.

Of course without the drug/money and the female users 'need' to use , he possibly wouldn't get a second glance, but instead of acknowledging this , he will continue to believe it is him super don , they are after.

For some men sex and crack are so interrelated that they won't have one without the other, they in a sense have 2 addictions now to tackle.

Crack becomes like a lover, it comes before their human partners, but their lover (crack) is one that only wants him when he has money, so he has to graft for her.

By the time he recognises he has a problem and reaches services for help 'she' has been working him good. I tell him he needs to recognise that he relates to crack like a seductive woman, whom is going to take him for everything his got. He needs to see the illusion she is creating. That he is 'The Man' she is playing him, she only wants him for money.

Men sometimes don't like this truth coming from a woman and may deny it, they can relate to what I'm saying (this is where it would be better if they heard it coming from a male worker , with me they think it makes them look sexist , and can be embarrassing for them.)

Obviously when men realise and accept this, then their ego is out to prove he has seen through her (Miss Crack), and she isn't getting his money anymore. Initially this is easy(ish), but again he underestimates her (miss crack), for in reality she isn't really a woman she is a drug, and this is where the next ego problem starts.

4, When they look at the size of a tiny piece of crack, 'how can something so tiny be so powerful over a man'? Thus the man has to go through the next stage , trying to get some control over the tiny bit of crack, now he has sussed her he is going to take control, and it often take time and money for him to accept he can't control crack , but the ego struggles all the way to prove different . As he underestimates how cunning 'she'/crack can get.

Additional male problems

For men crack can become intrinsically entangled with sexual gratification. Firstly as mentioned earlier men can feel like sexual dons, thus act upon these feeling/thoughts.

There is much misleading media coverage on crack making people feel very sexual, in reality for women this does not hold true, but for men it can often make them feel sexually aroused. The health problems occurs, in that even though crack brings on arousal because it's a stimulant it tends to prolong the erection, but becomes difficult for men to ejaculate as the penis seems to be over stimulated , thus men can develop sores on their penis , where they try too long. This puts them and others at high risk of contracting sexually transmitted diseases if no protection is used and someone is a carrier.

Men also report how they use sex as a tool for coming down from crack, thus entangled crack and sex even more.

Addiction for women

For women it is a different story

It's like they are in love with a partner that beats them. It is like they are in an abusive relationship, where their partner crack is beating them, controlling them, making them do things they don't really want to. They get vexed with them saying no more , but keep taking them back : Like abusive partners promise change, they come up with ideas about how seeing each other too often and if they saw each other less often they would get on. But like abusive relationships they try to see each other less but soon slip back into old ways; each time weakening the woman's self esteem.

Every time she tries to put an end to the relationship he stays away, gives some time and then promises her a good time. Just to beat her again. Crack plays the same game.

Don't underestimate the mind games the drug can claim.

Chapter 10 Seven types of users

7 types of users

You may have looked at other users and thought I am not like them but there are 7 types of users so it may be a good idea to know them to help you know yourself.

Type 1

Miss (Mr) 24/7

She /he do not stop piping, only in exhaustion; to sleep for couple of days, then 24/7 again. All activities in life are to get more crack. This type of user needs 24/7 support. If this is you, you'll need to find a drug free environment probably rehab. Some where you can eat drink and sleep to rebalance yourself.

Type 2

Miss (Mr) Daily

Miss daily knows she can't abstain, using every day, she may have tried to stop but only managed to stop for a short duration, with knowledge and support she may succeed without entering rehab.

Rehab isn't necessarily the answer; yes you get away from the environment but you need to learn to live in society. With all the stimulus's around. Use acupuncture twice a week, ideally every day.

Type 3

Miss (Mr) Binge

Miss Binge (not on a daily basis) wants to stop but attempts have failed. They usually use on pay day, given a survival plan in relation to the obstacles in the way and she/he can stop. They may deny addiction as not daily (see chapter 3 am I addicted?)

Type 4

Miss (Mr) Brandy on the rocks

She/he may drink alcohol with or without crack but if she uses crack she may use brandy to wash it down. Without crack she may or may not drink, individuals differ, depends on whether she drinks when not using crack or she may switch to alcohol to deal with crack cravings - fatal.

Miss Brandy on the rocks usually has a bloated face. Using stimulants with alcohol is very dangerous for two reasons firstly one is speeding up your body the other is slowing down and the body can get confused causing heart failure. Secondly using stimulants with alcohol can stop you feeling drunk yet the alcohol continues to poison your body without the normal warnings. Drunkenness is in really where the brain is becoming poisoned, that is what creates the feelings.

As long alcohol does not trigger crack cravings she can stop using crack first, then alcohol if she wants. If associations have been made in the brain; alcohol triggering crack cravings then alcohol has to go with the crack at same time.

Type 5

Miss [Mr] Ride a white horse -heroin

She has learnt to deal with the crash by using heroin as a come down tool, resulting in a physical addiction to heroin, but her first love is crack. She may get heroin substitute like methadone but needs work on abstaining from crack before cutting down substitute as cravings for crack will increase as she reduces. Once clean she may become over confident. Start using crack occasionally, and not want to believe she can relapse to old ways.

Type 6

Miss [Mr] Heroin rides out but can come home again

Favourite drug of choice Heroin, but sometimes plays with Miss White horse, (crack or cocaine) who gets her into more trouble, she's a bad influence. Her abstinence from crack may depend on what is happening in her life, she knows she's a bad influence, but plays with her if she comes round, or bored, frustrated with life etc.

Type 7

Miss [Mr] Seventh wonder of the world

This type just looks at the above and it just don't fit, the drug don't fit, maybe don't even like the experience of crack, don't want it, don't crave more, and don't know why they do it. May try real hard to stop yet always ends up back using again, determined to stop but don't.

At first it looks like someone may be using voodoo or something similar, and yes sometimes it is done on crack users, but also I came across mind control. May try real hard to stop yet always end up back using again. Determined to stop, but keep failing. This type is rare in my experience and took a lot to understand.

I have concluded now it is voodoo, Obiah, black magick whatever you want to call it or mind control or both, can be either or both.

The chances are if you feel your under attack from magick this possibly is the case; but you have no proof. There are things you can do, I will discuss in later chapters.

A way of identifying mind control is memory loss; pieces of memory missing, maybe pieces of memory that don't make sense or seem incomplete. Time loss you can't account for.

Sometimes even missing time is denied and not in awareness, but then if a person is honest with themselves they will know something just wasn't right growing up, they just don't know what.

So now you know why you're not like so and so, but how you going to stop!!!!! There are ways, what you got to lose?

Chapter 11   Dealing with cravings both physical and mental.

The first stage of your fight you will experience strong cravings coming in the form of smell, taste, voices nagging in your head to go and get some crack. This can last up to about a month after last use.

Basically because crack is a stimulant it has you spinning like a top can't sit still, can't stop thinking emotionally tense so the first thing you need to aim to calm yourself down.

Cravings and solutions

Craving for crack in two main forms:-

1, Physical - butterflies in the stomach, lung yearning.

2, Mental - Mind nagging to go and use.

Acupuncture

One of the most useful tools for this is acupuncture: not only will it instantly calm you down it will also take away the cravings, temporarily take away the nagging in your head and the yearning to use. It will relax you so that you can sleep or focus on what you need to do.

Now some of you straight away say 'I'm not having anyone

sticking needles in me, I don't like needles'.
Well firstly they are not needles they are little pins.

Do they hurt?

No, not really you get a pin prick at first then a sensation, which could be anything from itching, heat, dull aching etc. but it's nothing terrible and when you look at how much pain crack brings on you there's no comparison. Once the pins are in all the sensations stop, so whatever the sensation it only lasts seconds, then you relax for 20 minutes or so and become rapidly calm, peaceful; you may feel sleepy and by the end of the acupuncture session you will feel mellow, a little spaced out. Which is nice and no drugs included but a natural balanced feeling. The restlessness would have gone and the nagging in your head to go and get crack would have gone. Peace at last.

If you are still scared I recommended you watch someone else have it and see how they feel. At least try it before you dismiss it as it is one of the best known tools for removing cravings for crack.

How does acupuncture work?

Acupuncture is an ancient Chinese tool using needles in different places: either on the ear or on the body. There are channels running through our bodies like rivers and if there is a blockage in the river the flow cannot move easily the point at which the needle goes in releases the blockage and results in a steady flow of energy.

In addition to blockages there is a need for balance.

In eastern philosophy it is believed that the world, our bodies, everything is governed by 'chi' energy: chi is in all things and there needs to be balance in all things: yin and yang.

Ying and yang are terms used to explain opposite e.g., black & white, males & Female, hot & cold: our bodies need balance of yin and yang. We can become out of balance through things we do, our life activities, what we eat. Acupuncture puts us back in balance.

Crack is a stimulant so using it throws us out of balance: wound up tense, racing, whereas something like alcohol is a depressant slowing us down. In a sense sometimes we try to create our own balance by maybe using crack with alcohol or weed or heroin. Getting too manic so have a drink (alcohol) too sluggish take a stimulant. Acupuncture brings about balance between the yin and yang. The spaced out feeling experienced after acupuncture is really balance, but we are not used to feeling this in the stressful society of the modern world. Because you have been thrown seriously out of balance by using crack, when you first have acupuncture you won't stay balanced for long as your body is used to being manic, but each time you repeat having acupuncture the balance within you will stay longer.

How long will acupuncture last?

Auricular (ear)

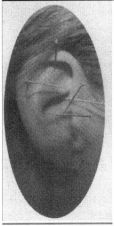

To begin with the effects of acupuncture may only last 20 minutes -1 or 2 days. Each individual is different. But let's say you're a one day person the first time you have it, the second time it will increase in length of lasting maybe 2 days. Ideally it would be good to have it every day for a few weeks, but whatever you have will be helpful in getting through the 4 week craving period, any at all is good!

If you stop using it will last longer each time. Remember it is helping you to keep you balanced and when you use the balance swings all one-way. Thus if you don't use you get better at staying balanced. Hence the lengthening of time after each pinning session.

Full body acupuncture

So far I have talked of acupunctures power and length of use with ear (auricular) acupuncture in mind. this is because most drugs services when offering acupuncture use ear acupuncture for its convenience in quickness of treatment; the treatment is mainly using 5 points (places) for the pins to go that have already been chosen as the best to use for drug users, so same for everyone , which is easier for workers to learn.

When we look at the whole body acupuncture performed by fully qualified acupuncturists, there is no one set of points for all people. The choice of which points are chosen to use will be decided based on the individual the doctor is faced with. They will look at the state of your whole health make up and decide the point's best suited to you. This diagnosis takes much longer and is far more skilled and complicated. The results expectedly of this level of treatment, the full body acupuncture treatment lasts longer. On the first attempt it can last maybe from 3-7 days; although it depends on the skills of the doctor in diagnosing and choosing which points to use, they have about 350 points to choose from. Many combinations of ways help but choosing which one to use is an art. For one point may work but another may work better. Anyhow full body acupuncture will last longer. If it doesn't I question is the doctor very skilled.

Money may play a very important part here, can you afford to go private or do you need to use the free service provided for drug users. If you can afford private I recommend you find an acupuncturist whom is Chinese, as their training is much more intense and they are more likely to think in the terms of eastern philosophy, translating what they understand into performing the art of acupuncture, with greater skills.

It will:-
- Reduce cravings
- Calms you down
- aids sleep

It may seem that all you need to do is have acupuncture, but no, acupuncture is only a tool, you have to work to get off crack. It's not letting you go that lightly. It will fight to keep you. It is like a relationship that is no good for you. You leave them, and then come back cos you 'love' them, you miss them. It's not going to let you go that easy, because you bring good money too. No you have got a fight on your hands.

Will I get addicted to acupuncture?

No! All acupuncture does is create balance, you can't become more balanced than balanced. If you gain balance through acupuncture and don't use crack, the balance will become naturally.

Chinese Herbs - Jei Wei Xaoi Yai Wah

There is a Chinese herbal medicine that was created specifically for heroin addiction (you can cold turkey with them). But they work for all drug addictions. It **detoxes** the body and **balances** it out; and with crack **reduces cravings** and ruins the buzz if you do use.

It come in bottles of little balls, these are fine but better still is those that come in little square bags (the Chinese herb shop may call them tea bags but they are not tea, but little balls you swallow). Take 2 bags in the morning and 2 in the evening. Reduce the dose to 1 bag if you're pregnant. They are quite strong on the stomach so the doctors would recommend you use them 6 days then rest for 1.

They are called **'jei Wei Xiao Yai Wah',** and are available in most Chinese herb shops. Usually sold for high stress, so works for that too. Usually they come in boxes of 10 or 30, they will sell them individually.

They:
- reduce cravings
- calm you down
- Help you sleep

Herbs do what acupuncture does but takes a little longer to get into your system, takes about half an hour.
Use both acupuncture and herbs if you can.

Strenuous exercise-Weight training

Your next tool is strenuous exercise

Strenuous exercise for more than 20 minutes will also satisfy cravings in a physical way. The chemical in your brain that crack releases to give you pleasure is dopamine and strenuous is exercise releases it too. Although not in the same quantities but you will feel a relief from craving.

It satisfies the receptors that are nagging for dopamine, which comes across in the form of craving for crack. The receptors in the brain are used to high doses of dopamine and exercise is a good way of releasing the dopamine in your brain.

If you've ever done exercise (which you probably have because most of you I have found have been good at sport in the past), you will know that you could of been miserable before you started but once you have broken a sweat you start to feel good and positive.

The receptors in the brain are used to large quantities of dopamine, this creates craving for dopamine and is satisfied somewhat by the physical activity. It also encourages the release of Norepinephrine which reduces depression.

So exercise feeds the receptors by shutting them up and giving you a positive buzz as well and gets you fit.

I say weight training because it is so strenuous but if you prefer another type of physical exercise that is fine it will still cause release of dopamine.

Weight training is good also because after stopping drug use people tend to concern themselves with their image more, women want to stay slim and men want to beef up. Weights bring a form of control on these matters. A feeling that most of us want to feel. But any form of exercise is useful, the more strenuous the better.

Exercise is safe and free and releases chemicals to reduce cravings; but can be used to get out anger and tires you out, and relaxes you to help you sleep.

Another beauty of helping yourself through exercise is that if in the middle of the night your cravings are intense you can do some sit ups, press ups or just dance to your favourite tune and this will help to reduce the craving.

- reduces cravings
- lifts the spirit out of depression.
- leaves you feeling in control

Alternative therapy

there are many alternative therapies available to help calm us down and that can only be a good thing, so if you would prefer a massage etc go for it, although I still recommend acupuncture and herbs to supplement other treatments.

In addition to the mental tools (below), acupuncture and weight training (strenuous exercise) there are various forms of alternative therapies that are useful in conquering cravings. There are also various herbs and specially designed teas on the market. Most drug services for crack users will offer detox tea, sleep tea and lung tea. You can also use jasmine/green tea to calm you down, also very good for cleaning nasty bugs out of body. Plus any calming oil such as lavender. Put the oil in a burner, in your bath on your pillow or cloths to inhale.

I also recommend using mineral stones for various purposes.
Tigers eye for protection from negative energy.
Smokey quarts to draw negative energy from your body.
Hematite for grounding if you're spinning holds it in your hand.

There are many other forms of therapies that can help calm you down reduce cravings. E.g. massage, reiki etc all are good.

Chapter 12 Mental cravings -mind games mental Tia chi against cravings

Ok so we have reduced the physical biological causes of craving. Leaving the mental cravings to deal with.

Go away go away go away.

The next step is to stop arguing with the crack nagging in your head. The usual situation is crack is nagging you to use. The crack won't shut up 'just one, just one, you're done so well just one'. The nagging goes on and on until you say, what the heck the nagging is driving me mad. I'll just have one. But it is easier to have none than one. So how do you deal with the arguing?

Mental tools

Crack has a very clever way of splitting the user's bad memories of crack (the crash) from the good memories (the high). Whilst they are separate Crack can run things. The last thing crack wants is for you to put good and bad experiences together. Thus the way to disrupt all her nagging tricks is to connect those separated aspects by making a link in the mind between the highs and the lows.

First stage: dealing with cravings

The first stage of your fight you will experience strong cravings, coming in smell, taste, voices nagging in your head to get some crack. This can last up to about a month after last use.

How to stop the mental cravings

As I said before crack isn't going to let you go that easy. Like an abusive partner, it will keep trying to get your attention. Nagging in your brain 'oh just one'. 'I've been good I haven't used for 'x' amount of time.' 'Just a little treat'. 'If I cut down'.

When fighting these mental cravings you will try and come up with the reasons why you shouldn't use. Arguing with the crack cravings in your brain, until the cravings won't just shut up! And often consequently you say 'I can't bear this any longer and if I have one the craving will stop even if it's only for a little while. So you decide to use. This results in chemical triggers in your brain telling you to use more. So one never means one. Unless you are out to prove you can and sometimes then crack lets you. By tricking you into believing you can get some control over the situation. And crack is patient like the devil and will let you con yourself you're in control so you don't fight so hard. Giving you a sense of false security. Letting you fool yourself. Crack lets people do this once even twice with relative ease but not much longer and you'll know this if you're tried.

The answer here with cravings of a mental nature is to **refuse to argue** with them when they come. Like when you finish with a bad lover. If you give them a chance to explain they'll suck you back in' even let you let off steam on them. They don't mind as long as they can get you back.

Don't argue with the cravings, don't discuss them or they will hook you into an argument and before long you will use just to shut them up! Arguing with will feed energy to the idea and it will grow. **Instead tell them to go away.** Don't give them the time of day. In whatever wording you like, but refuse to argue. Like with people you don't want to talk to, you just ignore them. And like a stuck record you say 'go away go away go away; and people do, they think 'She ain't going to argue with me I might as well go; because I ain't getting anywhere here. I'll try again later. That is what the cravings do, go away and try again later'.

Put another way, a child is nagging you for sweets. 'Can I have some sweets? I'd like sweets please'. If you were to argue with them saying 'No because.....' they would come up with reasoning around what you had just said. Going on and on until you give in to shut them up. If you tell the child 'no shut up asking' and that is all you say every time they ask, the child will give in, they can see there is no point to asking and intend to try you later when you're in a different mood.

Crack uses the same game, if you refuse to argue it says I'll try you again later and the nagging leaves your head; because it knows you mean it. The craving will leave for maybe an hour, maybe only half an hour and then return to try its luck again. On its return tell it 'go away', again. And refuse to discuss or argue. It will go again with view to come back, but sooner or later it gets the message. It isn't going to be able to talk you into using! Thus stops trying, that tactic! Yes that tactic. There are many tactics up cracks sleeve, but each can be conquered. The good news is the craving stage of recovery only last 4weeks; if you don't use during that time you move into the next stage.

Chapter 13 How to stop sensory/physical cravings

When dealing with sensory cravings like smelling it, tasting it, crack is being more subtle , it's no good telling these cravings to go away in word form as it isn't presenting itself in word form; it is coming from a deeper level of feeling rather than thoughts, so you must approach it as a feeling.

Physical craving

To deal with the physical craving you need to know they will pass, but meanwhile a way to get rid of them is to bring forward other physical feelings that don't want to be associated with. E.g. a painful memory /experiences you have had as a result of using crack.

Often the you will try this, but overdo it, by bringing up many bad associations. This only serves to distance you from the emotional elements of those bad experiences, as you are busy thinking of all the memories. Instead it is much better to think of **one bad** experience and try and bring forth the feelings you felt at the time. This experience you need to recall every time you have a physical craving.

To deal with cravings we need to go back to the earlier mentioned 'relationship' men and women have with crack. (Chapter 9 on Men and women).
For men Miss crack isn't going to let him go that easy; he provides good money and works hard to get it for her. When he tells her its over she will try many ways to get him back.

For women she earns good money too and so like a love r who just keep taking and when she has nothing left the abuses, so she keep providing to satisfy need.

Sometimes in abusive relationships we can hate the person. Saying 'I never want to see them again' and then after time we miss them. We don't remember or think of the bad they did, we just remember the good feelings we had and start saying we miss them, those good feelings. Crack somehow divides your mind. It seems to separate good feel memories from bad feeling memories. If you were able to remember bad feeling when you got good feeling memories you wouldn't use crack again for the bad feelings far outweighs the good feelings. So the feelings are blocked from being aware of each other.

For females liken it to an abusive lover turns up at your door (after you've decided to end the relationship). They come with positive vibes, maybe flowers or chocolates, on their best behaviour. Even though you may still have bruises from the last time; you see good feelings being offered. If you block out how you got the bruises or listen to the rubbish that comes out their mouth. 'I won't do it again'. Or you tell yourself we see too much of each other if I only see them once is.....' then we can just have the good bits. This again is crack patiently getting you to con yourself that you are in control. The truth is you let them in (partner or crack) for nice feelings and off you go again on the emotional roller coaster. So how do you end this trick crack has? Well as for the partner at the door you start to show them the bruises they left and they probably say I'll see ya later ' they don't want to go over the mess they left behind last time. They didn't come round for that; and it's the same with crack. If the positive emotions are exposed to knowledge of the negative emotions the positive ones will not stay around. For if they did they would become connected in your mind, both positive and negative together which would result in you being aware of both; thus seeing clearly not to use. Crack don't want that at any cost for it would ruin the tricks it plays , you wouldn't be too eager to use if you could remember the awful feeling crack leaves you with after a visit. So when feelings to use come knocking on your door, nose, throat, stomach. It is time to show them the bruises, in an attempt to link the positive and negative feelings it is no good here listing all the reasons not to use, for that's a mental process and you need to outwit on emotional drive. Instead take one example of how crack has left you in a bad state from your memory of many. Think of that one chosen occasion and to get in touch with how it felt, it is an emotional memory that will be your tool here. When positive feelings towards crack (emotional cravings) come or smell and taste linger, present them with the 'bruises', the one chosen feeling from the bad situation with crack. Hold that old feeling until the craving has gone; and it will go quickly. If it doesn't great the two sides are communicating all the time the craving is hanging around, but the craving will go and come back later. Until like with the mental cravings it gets the message.

So when dealing with cravings meet feelings with feelings and thoughts with thoughts.

There are also other tools available to you in helping to reduce /remove the cravings. Remember that cravings are not for ever, firstly they won't last long; especially if you use these tools, can be reduced from 20mins to seconds, and you will only experience for one month if you stay clean. Then the craving stage is over good bye cravings!

Chapter 14 dealing with depression, boredom and other factors involved in stopping

Boredom

Boredom is a major issue when stopping because you are used to dealing with boredom by using. The crack using life style is very busy one, involving finding money to get crack then time flies.

Removed from your life time may feel real slow. And what is there to do?

I can list loads of things but you know best. Boredom can be because you don't feel stimulated. And at different points of time we all want different things. Levels of stimulation ; sometimes a comedy on the telly may be fine, whilst at other times it's just boring , we long for excitement and again each person finds different things exciting.
You need to look to your past to see what these things were, if you don't have anything then you need to find something or boredom will cause you to return. Have a look at what's available.
Some people seek the adrenalin rush that crack gives, if this is you then look for things that bring that on, things like snowboarding , paint balling anything that is in a sense dangerous will bring on adrenalin . Maybe take up some sort of contact sport. Boxing, Judo. Whatever appeals to you. Channel your need for danger into something else. Try different things see how they feel. You need as many choices as you can find, boredom has to be beaten!

Plan ahead so you can have an idea of what you're going to do each day. Nothings written in stone, you can change your mind, but have a plan /goal so you don't find yourself at a loose end, drifting aimlessly and bored.

Fail to plan
and you
Plan to fail

Best plan when you're on an up, as when down everything seems boring.

Depression

What goes up must come down , because as explained earlier in chapter 4 crack causes the release of the chemicals in the brain that bring a feeling of pleasure and also those that are there to prevent depression. Once the drug has worn off you will find it hard to experience pleasure (as dopamine has been wiped out) and it can be hard to avoid depression as also wiped out Norepinephrine. You're in a no win situation. So what can you do?
The first thing you need to do is rebalance the brain, this can be done through the use of acupuncture and Chinese herbs. (Jei Wei Xiao Yaoi Wan) and also through things that you have in normal life. If you feel depressed a bath is always a good way of refreshing yourself soaking away all the negativity absorbed into your skin. Make it special if you can by putting lavender oils in it, lighting some candles have your favourite tune playing. This is a good thing to do when you're crashing after use also as the initial crash only last 20-30 minutes, then the worst is gone. So half an hour soak will help

you survive the black cloud time.

Crack induced psychosis

If you use a lot of crack it can bring about a form of psychosis: visual and auditory hallucinations. That is seeing and hearing things that are not there. You may feel you are mentally ill, you may be diagnosed as mentally ill and in a sense you are, temporarily. There is a difference though between normal psychosis; where people see and hear hallucinations. And crack induced psychosis; the difference is that with crack induced psychosis you are aware that you are hallucinating, you question what you see/hear is true. Crack induced psychosis is caused by chemical overload in the brain, give your brain a rest and it will sort itself out, rebalance. If psychosis does occur ideally stop using. Acupuncture will help greatly in encouraging the brain to rebalance. If you stop using the hallucinations should be gone within 6 weeks. If there do not I recommend you seek psychiatric help. You can ask for help before this although I know a lot of people are reluctant to, it is not necessary unless you feel you are a danger to yourself or others e.g. you may hear voices telling you to do something dangerous or harm another. Sometimes though the hallucinations are not life threatening e.g., you see a bee that isn't really there or snakes climbing you legs.

Exercise

Exercise is very useful as it encourages the brain to release the dopamine that you are craving. Thus lifts you out of the low feelings. It is good as you could take yourself off to the gym or to the park for a jog. But also you can easily do exercise in your home; some sit ups or press ups maybe. This tool is there at anytime you feel low or are craving. Some of your cravings will be caused by the brains yearning for dopamine that you were satisfying with the use of the drug now you need to satisfy it in natural ways, and your brain has got used to large amounts.

To get rid of the feelings of depression you need to encourage the brain to release dopamine naturally. In life without drugs one of the ways we produce dopamine naturally by doing things that bring pleasure for the chemical is our natural way of knowing something is giving us pleasure. You may have difficulty thinking of things that bring you pleasure especially when you are feeling depressed. Each individual enjoys different things so you need to look at what you enjoy. If you have been using crack for a long while you may have forgotten what you do like, try to remember back to what you used to enjoy. I will list some common things people enjoy here to start you off; you may or may not enjoy them.

Walking - Anywhere is good but maybe new places
Dancing - Find uplifting tunes
Reading - Builds concentration
Computers - Join library if haven't got one
Puzzles - Got to get your mind working
TV, videos - good to distract your mind
Meeting new people – You may need to meet new people,
                        Non using friends.
Snowboarding - Very thrilling but not everywhere
Cycling - Good for exercise and solves money

concerns
Writing - Releases tension and creativity
Playing music- Listening to music affects your mood
Making music/singing - Playing instruments lifts your mood

If you are feeling depressed you need to change what ever your doing, change your flow/vibration. As said before baths are always a good starting point. After that exercise even if you just have a little dance to an uplifting tune. Talking to positive people or writing out your feelings or some life experience can move you on. Try not to remain stuck as this will spiral you deeper into a darker place. Change something either what you are doing or environment. It is often good to change your furniture around or decorate to move away from the memories of using if you used it in your home.

Write the list of what you like/liked doing. (You may not remember all so add them when the memories come back). I say liked as you may not like them now but you may be able to find a branch of that interest stimulates you. It's about brain storming to encourage creative thinking of things you can enjoy. Also whether you think you still enjoy doing these things or not write all the things you enjoyed doing in the past; as when you are depressed sometimes nothing feels like fun. And you could be rejecting a good lead.

Make a list of all the things you need to do. Add to it as and when new things come up or you remember them. Tick the things on the list when they are done as this gives you a visual sign of achievements. They maybe large or small but they are achievements and an indicator that you are reclaiming your life.

Short term plan

8 day plan

Monday	Tuesday	Wednesday	Thursday
Acupuncture Get money	Jog	Go park	Visit library
Friday	**Saturday**	**Sunday**	**Monday**
Visit Friend	Go shopping	Jog	Acupuncture Get money

Basically start with the day you are writing it and write out what you need to do. add anything you would like to do. Be realistic when planning. The plan is to help you focus; if you don't achieve it all do not punish yourself with negative thoughts: just add them into your following weeks plan.

With your short term plan you need to fill up your days. Keeping busy keeps your mind off drugs.
Remember to include in your day you need **nutritious food**; for your body is probably deficient in many vitamins and minerals. **Exercise** to encourage the natural release of dopamine and lift/avoid depression.

Focus time for planning, get a routine. **Bath time** to refresh your body will remove negativity. Do one 8 day plan each week. Include things not done from previous week plan, add new things and keep busy.

Long term plan

You will also need a long term plan. You need to fill your time with bigger goals e.g. a job, study, hobbies, decorating etc. Your concentration may not be good to begin with but it will improve as time goes on and practicing doing something that requires concentration will help it improve faster.

Because it takes 2 years to fully recover from crack addiction you need to create a 2 year plan that is 24 months. To begin with you may not be sure what you want to do it may seem daunting, don't worry just put ideas down and fill it in as you go along, you can always redo it. It is just a good idea to have a vision of where you want to go. When planning bear in mind the stages you will go through. I will explain in next chapter.

In first 3 months focus on keeping busy and staying away from triggers, building a new life. You will do well to find work or hobbie or study plan.

Chapter 15 How am I going to get off and stay off?

(2 year plan)

So you've decided to stop crack, Hallelujah

Well I think you know already this isn't no easy task, crack is the most powerfully addictive drug I have ever witnessed. It's cunning and mind controlling: with many tricks up its sleeve, whilst potentially laughing at you every time you think you're getting away. Unlike heroin there's no physical addiction to remind you you're addicted. Some of you can convince yourself you're not! Therefore the drug goes through lives underestimated, so you don't see what it has in store for you. And when you wished to see it for what it is, it will change and adapt its behaviour accordingly.

This may not be nice to hear but it is so, it takes 2 years to fully recover from crack addiction, to be able to say your off. That is how patient the drug is. **That's not 2 years of hell** trying to recover but 2 years of trickery you have to be aware of and finding ways to foresee and avoid the relapse route crack sets up for you. **The craving hell only lasts one month** if you don't use, after which it's the tricks to get you back that you'll have to contend with. But here I'll show you the tricks and the ways to out manoeuvre them.

I hope you still with me and motivated to stop at this stage.

Two years probation, how am I going to get off? Starve the tree and escape

So you want to stop using, good I am pleased!
It isn't going to be easy, but it is going to be worth it!

Two years you see written and that may seem long, but that is how long it takes and that is why many people come off and go back, because the drug gives you an illusion you're free only with plans to get you later

The good news **is it will not be 2 years of struggle**. The struggle **only lasts 1 month,** yes only 1 month of cravings the rest is trickery. That is not to say the rest will be easy it won't it will just appear easy but really it is the hardest part because it feels easy too easy to believe, and that is the point never believe it is easy never underestimate the power of the addiction. It is the over confidence that brings you back.!!!

There are 5 stages you need to get through to escape cracks hold.

Stage 1,

4 weeks and no more craving!!!!! (Maybe 8 if you use only monthly; on payday)

The **first stage** is the cravings they must be reduced/removed
The drug puts up a fight like someone you're trying to get rid of in your life a partner maybe they aren't going without a fight they will pester you and pester you until you give in. for

women it is like an abusive partner who then comes with sweetness and charm offering you the world. For men it is like a seductive woman who wants to take you for everything you have; especially when she knows you have got money in your pocket she smells it and she is there. I know you can relate to these relationships because the nature of the drug brings these relationships into your life even if they weren't there before. It is like crack is more than just a drug; it has its own personality and creates it through you. And uses the traits to keep you in your place, addicted. But knowledge is power and knowing your enemy empowers you to predict their next move. It plays hardball but always in the same order, with similar tricks that I have witnessed again and again. Although if you go all the way through this 2 year process and decide later to start using again the game changes and becomes unpredictable so please do not get complacent once your free, thinking I did it before I can do it again.

Cravings

Cravings come in different forms: feelings, thoughts and nagging in the head. They are partly to do with the physical drive created in the brain and partly to do with learnt behaviour (conditioning) and the personality change/take over the crack brings. I have detailed how to deal with each type of craving in chapter 11 , 12 and 13.

Reducing cravings

Instant relief can be achieved by
acupuncture
Chinese herbs

Strenuous exercise-for more than 20 minute will also satisfy cravings in a physical way.

Alternative therapies
There are many other forms of therapies that can help calm you down reduce craving e.g. massage, reiki etc All are good

Money problems

If you are in a position where you can have someone hold your money for you, do so. For Crack knows the money is there and will nag you to spend it. If not try to put it in a bank so as to make obstacles in your way giving you time to think without spending it. You need to come away from all your crack using friends they may be lovely people but as a user they can't be truly themselves. If it means you have no one then so be it, you will need to make new friends.

Remember it is only for 1 month that you will get cravings then the games begin!

Plan you time – fail to plan and you plan to fail

During this month you need to also find something to do with this new spare time exercise is one thing but tiring and limited. Your concentration is not like it was but will return in time. You need to think of what you used to enjoy doing before you became 'friends' with crack and were taken off your life's path. One thing I learnt about crack users is they are players not plodders, they were destined to be high achievers maybe they weren't getting there fast enough and crack appeared helping to make them feel like they had already reached, but took them off their path. I suggest you try to write down all the things you liked doing wanted to do, sports you enjoyed etc for when you feel low you may not be able to remember but you could look at the list to remind yourself. Get back on track! Write out a plan for the following week and try to stick to it, if you go off track just start again. You need to retrain yourself to focus on achieving your goals boredom don't suit you.

By the end of the 4 weeks you should have some sort of routine and be clearer about where you want to go.

Sugar cravings

Remember as I said earlier, when you stop using you might find you have strong cravings for sugar, don't be alarmed. This is because crack raises your sugar levels and when you start to crave sugar as your sugar levels drop. It is quite common for people to want 6 sugars in their tea. Go with it as fighting against it will make you more moody. It should stabilise out in time and gradually your desire will decrease. You probably aren't carrying too much weight anyway.

Nutrition is important though as you probably are deficient in many vitamins and minerals especially vitamin C and B, as crack depletes these. Vitamin C is for skin, it stops it getting dry. It also helps to prevent colds. Vitamin b is for your nervous system it helps you stay calm.

Stage 2

Let the games begin

Second stage last 2-3 months

Remember I said the drug is like an abusive lover or a seducer, someone who wants to take you for everything you have. Neither gives up that easily. The first month they nag you continuously hoping you will break at some point. But you didn't (hopefully}, and if you did you just say I'll start again, I'm reclaiming my life! The Crack man [woman] in your head says ok so nagging won't work I'll try something else if I can't get you whilst you conscious because you know my game and are ignoring me, I will come when you're not alert/aware I will come in your sleep!

Dreams

so you managed to conquer the skills of resisting using as you get the cravings under control the lover in your brain isn't going to let you go that easily , you work hard for them you bring them good money. It can't control you in your waking life, so it comes in your sleep/dreams.

Here's the dream it is virtually the same for everyone. You are just about to light a pipe and you wake up. When you awake you feel as though it is real; your heart is pounding etc, the cravings to go and get some are intense.

You may dream you are just about to light a pipe when you wake up, your body believing in the dream will be ready for a rock. Excited and heart pounding you have major cravings you need to get through. You need to ride the cravings like a wave breathe deeply to calm yourself. Knowing they will rise then fall.

Put obstacles in your way to help yourself e.g. don't have phone on or at side of bed. Don't have enough money in easy reach. Just acknowledge the dream and its purpose and try not to give it anymore energy.

Avoidance tactics

You are a very powerful person if you put your mind to it, you can do what you set out to do.
The problem with going back to crack once you managed to abstain, it is due to overconfidence and consequently risky behaviour. Risking dangerous close proximity with the drug. This is what you need to master.

False confidence it's another one of cracks demonic traps. You must stay conscious to the fact that you need to avoid close proximity at all costs. walk miles to get from A to B ,going the long way round; not via danger zones, you must acknowledge this and be on guard, plan the occasion; bring non using companions , to reduce the risk , and do your thing, then leave. You've got no constructive reason to stay. You would walk miles around the houses if you saw a police man, you see them as enemy and crack isn't your friend.

For this stage you need to make sure you do not have money in your house, switch off your phone.

Stage 3
3 months clean you're feeling great; too great!

No more cravings, no more dreams, in fact you feel so good you can't believe you've done it. You feel like you will never use again, no desire to.
How comes it was so easy you say?
It isn't it's a trick!!!!!!

Remember that partner you want to get rid of, Crack man or miss seducer they tried nagging you, they left you be, came in your sleep whilst you was vulnerable. It didn't work. They are not letting you go that easily, they say erm! Nagging didn't work. Catching them vulnerable didn't either. Their too guarded. I'll let them feel I'm out of their life forget about me then come when they least expect it, when their guard is down!
You feeling so confident, why you've overcome the most addictive substance known to man, how could you not feel confident [erm over confident]. Don't underestimate the tricks of this drug, it's seen it all before and believes it's just a matter of time; it will patiently wait for an opening.
In fact I have seen many times it even give you the opening. Don't be surprised when you keep bumping into dealers and users. It will be offered you cheap on credit even free. You'll find money everywhere I've even had people find cash machines requesting how much they want to withdraw. You avoided these people to begin with but now you feel so confident you let yourself walk where you shouldn't maybe even to show yourself how well you've done. No no no no no! you are walking straight into the trap. I've seen people at this stage feel so much confidence they even go and sit with crack

users to in a sense show off how well they are doing, they come away so proud they didn't use. But this is the trick overconfidence, the drug thinks let them go on! No rush! You may do this once even twice but the third time it gets you, it's a game with your ego don't be fooled! Raise your self esteem for a positive aim. Showing you can talk with users, sit with users is not in your best interest. Stay away, avoid them and get on with your life. Where are you going? How you going to get there? Stay focused. The more focused you are on your goals the more crack will resign to wait; it knows your guards are up and the time ain't right, good! Gives you more time to get absorbed in your agenda. If you don't use at the 3 months point the drug will wait until 8/9 months has past then try again! If you do use don't say that's it I've messed up can't do it, and all that negative thinking. Say this was a lapse, I'll learn from it and start again. We learn from our mistakes.

Stage 4
8/9 months

Well done! You are now no doubt on track, probably working or studying. Crack users are always high achievers, wanting things yesterday, and usually get them. Ever determined to find a way. But careful here comes your old friend crack. It feels you are really doing well now and that's not good. Your guards are down the drug well out of your life, but remember this stage exists. Careful of parties etc the offers are coming from where you least expect, maybe someone has some cocaine [cracks cousin] it will still bring you back to crack. Maybe a joint laced with it.

Stage 5

18 months/2 years

You've nearly made it!
You know it and so does the drug, same tests as before. You feel like celebrating your success **careful! Don't let your guards down.**
Well done you've done it!!!!!!!!!!!!!!
You're in the clear please do not attempt to try and start and recover again because the game changes next time round and I can't simplify it in a book.

Stages of recovery an overview

Stage 1	Stage 2	Stage 3	Stage 4	Stage 5
Cravings Fisrt 4 weeks	Dreams 2-3 month	False sense of security 3 months	8-9 months Trick to test you	18-2 years Tricks to test you again

24 month plan overview

1st cravings	2nd Dreams of using	3rd False sense of sercurity	4th	5th	6th
7th	8th	9th Tricks sent to hook you back	10th	11th	12th
13th	14th	15th	16th	17th	18th
19th	20th	21st	22nd	23rd	24th ~ **Final tests**

Chapter 16 Different strokes for different folks

So now you know why you're not like so and so and how you going to stop!

But 7 types means some of you will need extra help

24/7 users need to find a safe drug free environment to rebalance your mind and body. This may be a rehab, but not necessarily can be a holiday destination away from users.

All users can benefit from acupuncture; some drug services offer it free usually auricular acupuncture [ear acupuncture]. The best in full body acupuncture but it isn't always available. If you can afford it go private.
Also use Chinese herbs.
Exercise.

Tools for the seven wonders can help all [it's elemental dear Watson]

These tools are to address any occult practices that may be being used against you, but even if that is not the case the natural aspects of these tools can aid anyone trying to gain and retain balance in natural ways.

Earth

You may feel like your spinning can't sit still, you need grounding the best way to ground is to touch the ground ;

walk on the earth at park, forest, or garden any land will do this will calm you down and put you in touch with yourself.

Air

Make sure there is a good air flow in your home. Again walking outside will help especially by the sea.

Fire

Incense stick can help to cleanse the air in your home use calming scents like lavender or frankincense and myrrh. If you feel you are being psychically attacked use 4 candles in each direction of the room; north, south east and west.

Water

A soak in the bath is very good for calming down, if you feel cold inside it will help warm you, to cleanse the water you can use salt.

Spirits and demons

It may bother some people that I include this area into this book but it does affect some people's lives and is rarely spoke about. It is a hidden area. Whether you believe in such things or not some 'Crack houses' are set up by people who use occult practises in addition to dealing crack. Some users express to me a strong pull for them to go to those buildings to buy, even though they truly don't want to. The drugs no different and the environments are far from friendly. It is believed that crack or any stimulant opens up your chakras for demons to enter. When some people try to get clean they experience a fight that can take many forms from illness to shaking fits. Sometimes this makes them feel like they don't want to stop to deal with this, but there is ways so don't give up.

If you do believe you are under some sort of **psychic attack** it is worth knowing that everyone has a spirit guide that can help them at any time with many things but you need to ask for their help as they have to respect free will. You don't ask they can't help. Psychic attack is usually on your chakras {you have 7 main ones on your body}. They can protect you in a shield which repels the attack, and aid the clearing of your energy field.
This is a simple way to ask.

I call on my spirit guides to come forward
And close down all my chakras completely
Disperse all negative energy
Seal a gold cross on the top of my head
Fill my body with gold light
And surround me in a shield of protection

Crack/stimulants the opening of the third eye [one of the 7 chakras]. It is through the open chakra that entities can enter. To some of you reading this book it may seem a silly idea don't worry just focus on stopping. For many I know I need to cover it because no one else will for fear of criticism.
If you feel you do have a resident entity you need to call on a higher power to remove it whether it's Jesus Christ (for Christians} or whoever is equivalent for your religion I'm

sorry but I don't know whom they are. You may not be strong enough and clear in thought to do this alone. You could go to church to ask for deliverance although not all churches are what they say they are. Alternatively someone clean and positive could ask with you.

You could say something along these lines

In the name of Jesus Christ our lord I ask for deliverance.

To help yourself for all sorts of psychic attack you may find it beneficial to say this written below 3 times morning and night for 21 days

I disconnect from all cording binding's imprints overlaps and possession
that does not serve my highest purpose at this time
I disconnect now

I reclaim my personal power from all times and all dimensions that will
serve my highest purpose at this time
I reclaim it now

I decree in the name of God that any of my power and abilities that have
been copied and stolen are returned to me now
And that all copies be destroyed
I decree this happens now

Grounding

Using crack you will find it hard to stay grounded, under any sort of psychic attack you may also find it hard to ground. You may be so hyped up you can't calm down? Maybe you don't want to calm down; you enjoy these highs. You want to keep them fine. You can but if you learn how to ground yourself you can fly towards your chosen destination rather than be propelled so fast you find it hard to focus, you can't do this if you're not grounded. You will keep being dragged by another current. To steer you need be grounded, to feel your feet on the ground. Yet your hands free to fly. You are in control by keeping a firm footing in reality.

Grounding tools

Gardening
Meditation
Yoga exercise
Stones
Incense
'Acts of faith' ((read)
Music ambiance
Time management
Counselling
Petunia
Protection rune
Candles
Lavender
Structure
Spiritual prayer
Writing down

Diary
Acupuncture
Walking
Calming teas
Chinese herb

This is a list I have made of things I have found good for grounding tools, you can make your own or pick from this list. Choose one from the list start doing them adding them into your daily program and life will become less threatening of walking or flying into danger. You will find peace and consequently feel in control of your destiny.

Dealing with mind control

If you can relate to what I'm saying about loss of memories or time loss you can't account for there are things you can do to help yourself.

The first thing you need to do is get a watch so you can keep yourself aware of time. And aware of time loss, when and how long for etc. By being aware of time you also reduce the amount of time you lose.

Retrieving memory is possible for everything you experience is stored and can be retrieved. The best way to retrieve memory is to write down all you can of each memory, it may seem blocked but bear with it, relax breath deep and go deeper inside yourself and try different ways of accessing it. Think about other aspects of the memory e.g. smells, weather, season. How old were you, what were you wearing, what happened before and after. Some memories you may question were they real, write them down, what happened before and after and come back to them maybe a 3 week later if they are the same you will know if they are real; truth doesn't go away. I know it is easier to talk about them but don't as they can become muddle and if they were traumatic they can cause an unnecessary emotional reaction, reliving the experience again. By writing you don't have to relive the trauma, the process of writing connects the memory to the left brain, making sense out of what may seem nonsense, allowing you to move on. After you have written out memories you could show them to someone you trust, they could read them and ask you questions about it, but again do not answer verbally; write it down. The questions they ask should not be leading questions, suggesting anything as this can contaminate/confuse your memory.

For more in-depth understanding of the nature of mind control and how to deprogram read
"ACCESS DENIED for reasons of National security"
O'Brian& Phillips ISBN 0-9660165-3-x [not easy to purchase but available
through their website www.AccessDeniedBook.com.

Kathleen Sullivan 'unshackled'.

'Deeper insight' by Fritz Springmeir and Cisco Wheeler.

But know that these books can be triggering for those whom have been mind controlled and also may scramble your memories.

Chapter 17
What about pregnancy

Crack use and pregnancy

This is an extremely controversial area, some claim terrible effects others dismiss them as caused by other factors such as poor diet, lead poisoning, stressful living conditions. I am not a doctor so I may not completely understand all factors involved, but I have read material on the issues etc. My experience in England has been that I haven't seen any negative results in the children born to crack using mothers, I have seen other professionals change their views of what they observe since they were informed that the mother had used crack. I have read reports from the states that claim many serious concerns. I questioned why I wasn't seeing these claims myself. . I was lucky enough to work for some time with an ex-user who now wanted to help, she was from Brooklyn and I asked her why I was not witnessing the same as claimed by USA reports shaky babies after birth. I asked all my clients if this was so with their babies and they said No'. I asked my Brooklyn girl had she seen any shaky babies. She said yes. We looked for the reason why it wasn't the case in England. She suggested the amount the mother used was a factor; it was cheaper in the states and so people used more. I had a client that was partner of a dealer, she used enormous amounts per day, yet still her baby wasn't shaky when it was born. My Brooklyn girl suggested that life style was also a contributing factor; my client was nicely housed and ate well. Here we have money for unemployed people but in states not always so. It seems the shaky baby seen in the states is a result of large amounts of use coupled with poor living conditions and malnutrition.

Many of the effects claimed to be caused by crack use can be accounted for by many other factors. It depends on which research you read. The only thing that seems to be a fact is that crack like any stimulant increases heart rate etc creating an environment in the body like that of stress; which restricts the blood flow through the placenta reducing the oxygen and nutrition supply to the foetus. Thus increasing the chances of miscarriage at any time in the nine months. The pregnancy is divided into trimesters meaning, three monthly parts. In the first trimester it can cause miscarriage, in the second trimester it would be a still birth and in the third trimester it would cause premature birth.

Depending on how often the mother is using the size of the baby at birth may be affected, they may be small.
Research shows that premature babies are more prone to suffer in later life from cardio-vascular problems.
If you wish to find out more about the research findings on using crack whilst pregnant I recommend a book called ' Cocaine - exposed infants social , legal and public health issues by James A Inciardi , Hilary L Surratt, Christine A South Sage publications ISBN 0-8039-7087-0

Chapter 18 Disease model addressed (who gets hooked)

There is a belief that some people have addictive personalities. It is this belief that is behind the (something) anonymous groups, e.g. AA Alcoholic anonymous, NA Narcotics anonymous etc. I personally have issues with their beliefs although it works for many people and if it works that is only good. But for some people it isn't suitable. The 'something anonymous' belief is that some people are born with addictive personalities and therefore they become addicted to many things , it isn't their fault so instead of struggling with their addiction , blaming themselves they are advised to ask a higher power for help and stay away from all addictive substances or life styles. The problem I see with this belief is that many people hear about those people with 'addictive personalities' and decide they don't relate to that, believing therefore those who become addicted to crack have addictive personalities and that isn't them so they won't get addicted.

But they will, **after 6 months anyone** who uses crack over that length of time will become addicted it doesn't matter whether you have an addictive personality or not, the drug is addictive and will change your brain accordingly. With the belief in the addictive personalities existing we are in some way encouraging people to use, those whom know themselves to not get addicted to say alcohol will feel safe trying crack. Not good because if they keep using and they will become addicted.

Pharmacology treatment is a no no

Some drug services and doctors prescribe various drugs, sometimes anti depressants, tranquilisers to help you sleep or more serious drugs to help deal with hallucinations. Yet most probably the symptoms you are taking them for are caused by crack use. You may feel you need them but then they can be addictive too. So I recommend instead of asking for these drugs to be prescribed, use alternative treatments offered here in this book. If you are already being prescribed drugs ask your doctor about reducing or stopping.

Considering Narcotics anonymous

I do think Narcotics anonymous (N.A.) helps all people. I do think asking a higher power for help is a good idea, but I don't think it is essential to enable someone to stop. The same with using other substances or living a certain life style. N.A. would insist you give up all addictive substances or lifestyles. Some of my clients have had difficulty with this or don't want to stop all drug use. I have found that some people do have to stop using all substances or lifestyles; whilst some can continue to smoke cannabis or drink alcohol. It depends on the individual. It seems some crack users make connections in their brain with crack and other substances, e.g. cannabis. If they smoke some it increases their cravings for crack, they have made an association. If this is the case you can't use cannabis. You will end up using. If you haven't made the association then it is possible for you to carry on using. With life styles sometimes people steal to raise money for use, often when they stop they try to continue their money raising activities but this can also be associated with the drug and as they get enough money they start to crave. You must be honest with yourself; in order to stop using.

N.A. meetings can help you as you will get support from the group and sadly there isn't much of an alternative to these group. This is fine if you fit in and stop all but if you wish to continue using other substances, it can be a problem.

Chapter 19   What about heroin, methadone, weed and alcohol

Some of you use other substances to; you may or may not want to stop using those as well. Well the reality is some of you can continue using them, whilst others may not. It depends on what associations crack has made with them. That is sometimes the brain has put the 2 substances together, you can't use one without the other. E.g. some people don't use weed say when they used crack so there is no association. If there is an association made by using weed and crack a craving to have some crack will occur when they smoke weed. In this instance the person cannot have weed; as it induces crack cravings. Also substances like alcohol can reduce you resistance to fight cravings.

Sometimes people are addicted to more than crack, they may feel they want to stop everything but which drug first. E.g. if you have a heroin addiction also you may be finding by reducing heroin you use brings stronger cravings for crack. Often the same with methadone addiction; when you reduce the methadone the cravings increase for crack. The answer is to stop using crack first, and then reduce.
If your strongest addiction is to something other than crack stop using crack first.

If other drugs come after crack e.g. use alcohol/heroin to come down. By stopping your use of crack your need for alcohol etc will be reduced.

Chapter 20 Spiritual tools

This is an important area of recovery. It is important to think positive for with our thoughts we create our reality. Like attracts like. It is sometimes hard to think positive when our feelings are low, but remember they are low because the brain is lacking in dopamine, the more you do to aid production of it the quicker the low feeling will fade. Thinking positive also aids the production of dopamine and the reverse is going to happen if you think negative. Take control of your feelings and your thoughts. Maybe write down some positive affirmations. Put them on the wall where you can see them. It is said that if you say a statement 21 times it brain washes you to think it. Try it with positive affirmations. Remember to avoid saying negative thoughts; it would reverse your thinking. Think of what you want to achieve, and then write it, draw it, make it become a reality.

There are some good books out there with positive daily statements, written in short scripts; so not needing lots of concentration. My favourite is 'Acts of faith' by Iyanla Vanzant, ISBN 0-671-86416-5. It is a small book with a short reading for each day of the year and an affirmation for each day. I had a client (one of my favourites) she was a 24/7 user, and come in to me to get some housing support. She was in a bad way, but didn't want to stop at that time; saw it as too hard. I tried all manners of ways to convince her it was time but no not yet Lou was her reply. I gave her this book and made her an appointment to see a college the next morning. I told her be on time as she was a strict worker; not like me. My clients could just turn up and I would see them. This client never made it to appointments, wanted to but always got taken on a using path. The next day I came to work to find she had attended on time. Later that day she had a scheduled appointment with me, and she arrived on time. I asked how she did this. She said she had been up all night reading the book, and had arrived at our project before it had even opened. I thought this book is good! And from then on I provided it to all my clients, they love it.

Instructions on listing, factors that will trigger cravings.

Write a list of things that trigger cravings and remove what you can from your life. E.g. safety pins, coke cans. Avoid walking near dealers, go another route, the walk is good for dopamine production anyway. Add to the list any triggers as they become apparent to you.

write list of issues you have e.g. homeless , court case, outstanding bills, as you go through them cross them out to indicate to yourself you are achieving.

Help available

Where ever you live there will be some sort of help available, check your local directory for services or phone the national drugs helpline. Different areas develop different structural ways of helping drug users. Usually there is some sort of help for housing and support.

<u>Glossary</u>

Neurones = nerve pathways in the brain

Synapse = The point at which messages are transferred from one point to another.

Vesicle = Little sac's carrying neuro-transmitters

Neurotransmitter = Chemical that passes messages around the brain

Dopamine = a neurotransmitter that brings a feeling of pleasure

Norepinephrine = a neurotransmitter that indirectly prevents depression

Hypothalamus = Area of the brain that governs eating, drinking and sex drive

Reticular formation = area of the brain that governs arousal, alertness and attention

Arousal = alert, lively , aware

Pseudo-cholinesterase = an enzyme that breaks down cocaine

Cerebral haemorrhage = a stroke; where the blood vessels in the brain burst and blood goes into the brain

Hyperpyrexia = overheating

Autonomic nervous system = the nervous system copes with stress by speeding most bodily functions up to enable us to act fast ,in a sense it is sympathetic to our needs , gets us ready for 'war'

Para-sympathetic = is when the autonomic nervous system calms the body organs down to help us rest , gets us ready for 'peace'

Central nervous system = The brain and spinal cord go to make up the central nervous system

Reading list

'Women and crack –cocaine'
by Inciardi, Lockwood ,Pottiegar
 MacMillan press 1993.ISBN 0-02-359440-3.

'Women and substance'
by Elizabeth Ettore 1992
 MacMillan Press

'Women Drug users: An ethnography of a female injecting community'
 By Avril Taylor 1993.
 Clarindon Oxford

'Acts of faith'   daily meditations for people of colour
 By Iyanla Vanzants ISBN 0-671-86416-5.

'Cocaine –exposed infants social, legal and public health issues'
By James a Inciardi, Hilary L Surratt,
Christine A South
Sage publications
ISBN 0-8039-7087-0

Additional information on me.

I have added to this book the first 5 chapters of another book I am currently writing that exposes the corruption that goes on throughout our social structure that I have been witnessed to. Which caused much delay in providing you with this information/book.

By telling you of my life path I can reveal the darker sides of hidden truths.

There is currently more written up and placed on the net in blog and video form; under Higher Insight.

My web site is www.higherinsight.co.uk

Who is Louise Clarke?

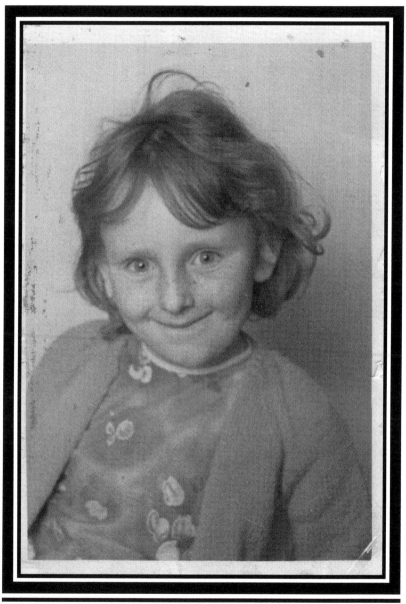

Who is Louise Clarke

Chapter 1   'It's here'

I feel the need to write this book but have no real structure in my head, as I write. I feel an urgency to write it off the top of my head, to accompany my book that I am currently finishing, 'Stop using crack and reclaim your life'. My knowledge built on years of experience has been put as clearly as I could into a self help book for crack/cocaine users. People may want to know how I gained this knowledge and insight and also may wonder how come I don't work anymore in the conventional sense of the word.

I decided to write this book therefore to accompany the other and due to the knowledge I am giving out I may not be able to do it at a later date. So as a consequence of my life's path which I have followed or more so been guided down, I am currently placed in a position of nothing else to do. I am homeless in a little sea side village, staying by the human courtesy /hearty acceptance grace of god. Call it what you will, in a lovely bungalow very near a desolate sea. I have an unfit dog to accompany me and my life basically consists of writing, walking, going in the sea. Taking photos and doing Sudoku. Beyond that my brain is vacant; therefore I cannot really concentrate on TV, DVD, books etc. I can have an intellectual conversation, but nothing that requires any memory cells, they are currently on overload. I therefore saw the opportunity to release them onto paper and the subject matter may be of interest to many.

Where to start? At the beginning, I suppose. I was born 1961, grew up on a housing estate in East London. And was seen as a naughty child, who did as she liked. This was true I suppose I wasn't nasty, but I did do as I liked.

I didn't like doing work at school, so didn't.

With knowledge now I know I was dyslexic. So that is probably why I didn't like doing any work. I remember age 6 writing a story, which our teacher gave us sweets for, if story was good. I didn't get a sweet, she said I hadn't tried. But I had, so I couldn't improve on the story, and had been diddled out of a well earned sweet. I decided I wasn't going to try anymore, what was the point, from then on I refused to take part in any writing activity. By age 7 in came the authorities, telling my Mum they wanted to put me in reform school. It was that or visits a psychiatrist regularly. She opted for the second option.

Can't remember him doing much therapy, just IQ tests and vaguely remember him insinuating I was stupid and that was why I didn't do any work. So I wrote a 21 page story about a haunted house, on a hill. To prove my intelligence; then went back to refusing. The solution was to give me clay to play with whilst the other children did the lesson. I then wasn't disruptive and that was enough for them.

Come age 10, time to move on to next school, I was told I didn't need to come and see him anymore. I didn't really like that decision, as I quite liked seeing him.

At the next school I just went back to doing as I liked. I was very good at Maths; mental arithmetic but I never wrote the answers down; just shouted them out as the teacher wrote the sums on the board, it infuriated them, and the class got the answers.

The end of the year, much to the disappointment of the teacher and the swot girls, I came top of the class. And 6th in the school, with 98% for maths. They decided I was good at maths , but because of the way things ran in school in them days , was same grade for Maths as English , give or take a grade ,I couldn't be in the top groups , as I couldn't spell., didn't write nor read. So the solution was I would need 'special work' but stay in the same class the following school year. But oh , I was with a new teacher who didn't anticipate my arrogance, when I told her I needed special work, she told me it wasn't going to happen and it didn't. So I just continued on as normal doing what I liked.

I went on to senior school, not allowed anywhere near the O'level classes, I was placed in grade 4, for maths. I at that time decided no I wanted to take O'level, but grade 4 didn't teach it. So I asked that I was put up. Due to my disruptive behaviour I was told I would need to behave first, this I did for a month , but to no avail, I thought oh you are just playing with me, you will never put me up , you just want me to behave, so I went back to my fun life style. Consequently I was placed in group 6. Here they knew nothing. It was sad but the teacher for that class was the head maths teacher. I asked for a deal , give me an exam , and if I'm good put me up to O'level class , this he did but put me in grade 4 again, to assess my behaviour. Basically the time past and I was not taught the maths O'level material. So CSE's it was, I got 6 CSE but they weren't really worth Jack. So I left school and worked in shops was a sales assistant. Bored, patronised and un-stimulated. I decided no more selling; I wanted to work in an office. But I couldn't type do shorthand or spell. I was sent to a print room of a chartered accountant, by a temp agency. And there I stayed for 3 years. The fastest collator they had ever had, but mentally under challenged. Bored by its futility, an opportunity arose to go to live in Gloucestershire, I took it. Took a while to adapt to the slow pace of life and find myself a path, and I realised I liked psychology. I found this out via finding a book in the library by Desmond Morris on animal behaviour, with many picture, I just loved it. Took note of the section it came from, 'psychology', and chose some more books, only to find they were written in another language 'academia', I wanted to read the books but didn't understand the words, it was hard work with a dictionary. So I returned to London to study psychology. I was planning on doing O'level because of the struggles I had with education and the prejudice received from being unable to read and write to well. I thought at the time very clever people did O'levels, but this wasn't to be. A new tenant moved into the bedsit where I was living, whom was extremely academic and told me no not to do O'level, as I would be extremely bored. I would do better to go for a level. So I did.

Wasn't completely simple as my life never is, but then I accept I choose the abstract ways. To get onto the psychology A level course one is required to have O'level maths, to be able to do statistics, which I had never done. I suggested as it was a two year course and O'level maths would be extremely easy for me to learn, I would do it the following year. Basically I blagged. Because I didn't really see the need to have O'level maths, just needed to be able to understand the maths related to psychology, mainly statistics. They accepted my offer but refused to help me during the course when I did find statistics hard. But I found a wonderful book 'statistics without tears', which basically explains how the statistics work logically so it became easy. Phew! I got told off for not writing anything down as they spoke, but I felt I was being very good, listening, paying attention, after about 3 months I learnt the skill to listen and write at the same time. I no longer was perceived as disruptive , as an adult my questions were valued , whereas as a child I was told to stop contradicting them, and when I asked 'what does contradicting mean' the teacher said ask my Mother.

Sometimes I would say what happened in the research and the lecturer would tell me to stop reading ahead, but the truth was most outcomes from research were predictable.

When it came time for entering the exam, I said I wasn't intending to, I just wanted to know the words; to be able to read the books in the psychology section. The lecturer insisted I entered for a degree in psychology, which I did. They asked I got a 'D' to enter, I got a 'B' I was in.

I was apprehensive about doing a degree, now they were really clever. I felt I was in right over my head but persevered. And I was ok after a while. Only problem was it was 1986 - 1989 and I am a lesbian, and those were prejudice times. We have changed a lot since then.

But as a consequence of prejudice, I noticed that much research in psychology never took into account sexuality, nor class for that matter and therefore the result for social psychology research were not all that they claimed to be. This annoyed me and in addition I was expected to write that everything is good to enable me to get good marks, my opinion was not valued, only published material is of value.

But fate allowed me some slack on the matter, so I decided I wanted to give a lecture to the lecturers on the issues of classism and heterosexist, and how I felt alienated in the university setting along with a small minority of others. I did this lecture whilst I did my final exams, it was a way I could balance writing things I didn't fully agree with in an exam, whilst expressing openly the truth , the whole picture of my experience and thought on the downfalls in research. On completing my lecture, the lecturers who attended were very impressed and amongst them was the editor for the Women's section of the 'Journal for the British Psychological society' (1989). She offered me that if I could write my speech as a paper within 6 weeks she would publish it. I did and it was published; now others have a publication to cite these views. I called it 'Academic Aliens'.

On completing the degree, I got a 2/2 with Honours. The examiners complained, apparently saying psychology was not political and some of us had made it so. I think I got marked down. Still I tried and I could only compromise a little. In those times they loved behaviourism. (It was a cheap solution) me I loved Freud and he was a dirty word.

The lecturers asked me what was I going to do, I said work with children on drugs; they said there was no such job. Oh I though.

But in time I did become one of the first drug counsellors to enter into schools in Britain to offer drug counselling to children.

Chapter 2 Becoming a drug counsellor

After finishing my degree I wanted to learn counselling but I wasn't entitled to anymore grants, I had seen a course I wanted to attend but it was £3,000 I decided I would need to make some money fly pitching in the street , it was winter so I decided to sell gloves and scarf's, I was doing ok until Christmas arrived and the police clamped down on the fly pitchers, I don't condemn their actions as there were too many people selling something but consequently I was unable to get the funds for my chosen path. Becoming depressed by the fact the benefit agency called me in, I needed to do some community development or whatever they called it then, basically I told them I wanted to learn counselling and get certificates needed. They said they would pay but I would need to be a volunteer somewhere and find my own placement. This I put off, but the certificates were two, one for skills and one for theory. I finished one and the benefit agency said they wouldn't fund the other one unless I found the required voluntary work, I had 2 weeks. I looked in Thompson local there was one drugs service , so I phoned them for an interview, my friends suggested I try other services but I insisted no if they don't want me , no one will so I am only trying the local one.

I attended the interview , was asked about my experience , I told of how when I street traded previously with badges; where many skin heads hung out ;to meet and sniff glue, I had just by nature tried to hear them and reason with them and supported them to stop. I also had previously had a partner whom met me as they were coming off; cold turkey from heroin. He liked me and asked when I wanted to start; I said I have to start in a week, to stay on my training course. This I did in 1991.

 I had noticed on the gay scene how many people took drugs and had alcohol problems. I also noticed that they didn't attend services, once I started working at the service I soon saw the prejudice by some staff towards gay people and even the resistance to address the issue, which I kept raising , consequently an ignorant member of staff objected to me keep going on about gay issues. When I insisted we monitor how many gay clients we actually saw, they argued if that was to be happening we should measure married people to. Therefore I had in mind to make lesbian and gay needs my agenda.

But no fate chose differently for me. Very soon after starting my voluntary work there, a woman came storming in the door, saying 'I'm a crack head. Someone better see me now. 'Everyone disappeared I was alone, I said I don't know anything about crack but would try and help her if she wanted. She agreed, so we went upstairs to a counselling room, I asked her what she wanted, she said she didn't want rehab but wanted to come off in the community, after assessing her use, it didn't seem very likely but I agreed with her to try it her way; but if it didn't work she agreed she would then try rehab. I arranged for her to see an acupuncturist, (I previously had a partner who was an acupuncturist and believed it would help). During the time with her my employee popped his head around the door, he spurted' don't bother with her she has got no ears', and his tone was jokey but serious. Apparently he had tried to help her previously by offering her rehab, but she refused to go; she had children. I arranged for her to come back in a couple of days after seeing the acupuncturist; to see how she got on. After a couple of days she arrived, but she said never did get there she did try, she got a cab but then diverted to dealer on the way. But had returned and now was willing to try rehab. My boss was shocked, to see her arrive; she usually only came in once about every 6 months. So he in shock asked how did you get her to come back, she never comes back. You must have something special. He now wanted me to focus on women crack/cocaine users and offered to employ me to do it as a job.

At that time nowhere else in the country was running a service for Women crack users; not really for crack users either. There were crack users even visible on the street the drug had been marketed since about 1986/87 but they didn't use services and services didn't go out of their way to get them. The truth was they felt inadequate with crack users, for with heroin at that time, we gave methadone, so the clients tend to tell you you're the best and don't put their dose down. They have something to come to you for and we have something to give them. So the worker is left feeling powerful, but with crack the worker knew of nothing they could give them, so felt inadequate and instead of getting praise from the client they could be condemned for being of no use. So consequently services didn't rush to draw into services crack users. There was no funding being made available Funders couldn't see a problem. Clients weren't using services, so no need for funding. My boss had worked with some crack users but recognised that females could be very seductive towards him to try and have things their way. So now he chose to give them to me.

The initial client I saw then went onto the street telling users about me and soon they were coming in insisting they saw Lou.

A man eventually turns up, but insisted he was smoking cannabis a lot and nothing else. It didn't make sense to me because I have met many cannabis users and know how their energies felt, but this guy it felt like I was choking , I ask a few times are you using anything else," no just cannabis." I excused myself and rushed downstairs to my boss, I told him I can't handle the client , I felt like I was being strangled . He would have to do him. He said no, the guy must be a crack user, and I told him no he is insisting he just uses cannabis. He said no that is how some men felt. Go back up and work with him. It was hard for I was scared of the feeling, but did it. Another crack using male came and again I felt the strangling feeling, after that I no longer picked it up the feeling, I just became able to sense a male crack user in a way. I continued on working with both men and women really.

The information available to me to learn from at that time was very little. A couple of books from the states, viewing it from a medical, academic view point not really telling you how to work with users. My boss had some experience of working with crack users so passed some knowledge onto me. And that was it really; the rest was up to me to work out.

Meanwhile the media wanted to cover the topic and because we were the only service seeing users in London and beyond, they insisted coming to me; they claimed I was an expert. This title worried me for I did feel like an expert, but who else would they go to, so I decided I would become an expert and study every aspect of the drug I could.

I ran a group made up of female crack users and ex-users and partners of users. Together we created informative cards for users and partners of users. But I tried to have it written by the users, they took 3 years to create because crack users in my experience do not do well in groups. They compete and have self esteem issues; therefore they are better off with individual counselling and treatment.

I continued learning all I could about crack users and in 1995

I was asked to speak at the first women and drugs conference ever held in England and possibly the last. I called my speech 'Run around can't get a rehab'. Which went down well and I was deliberately emotive, after which John Major put up £16 million for crack services for users. Then everyone suddenly could see users in their neighbourhood. I was asked by SCODA for the paper I presented at the conference, but it wasn't in paper form, I just had guideline notes but I wrote it up in a similar vein, and titled it 'The catharsis of women and crack'. It was printed in a 'Drug link ' journal and now can be found in many different languages on the internet.

In the speech I outlined the experiences of a female crack user and the obstacles that existed within our system that prevent entry into rehab and services; to be honest things have not improved since 1995, now it is extremely difficult for this client group to get anywhere near a rehab or suitable services.

I also started in 1995 training other drug workers in how to work with women crack users on intensive day training. Due to John Majors funding arrival the service I worked for was able to set up and offer a day care service for crack users, here I set up weight training for clients and found it was welcomed by both male and female clients.

I also spoke at a conference held in Euston, London (1996) by Women's Aid, 'Women drugs and violence'. This time I explained the predicament women crack users were in and then systematically went through the list of services set up to help the public and showed how each was failing her. I was raw I wanted to be to drive the truth home, but I think after that I was prevented from speaking any more , which I will come across later.

Then in 1997 the structure changed in our funding system, throughout the care professions, the health authorities now required accountability for the public monies they were putting into services.

I didn't like it one bit, prior to this I had been told by an ex-crack user from the states that the reason I did so well with my clients was because services were not compulsory, she told me how in the USA drug users did not attend services of their own free will, they were actively ordered by courts to attend, which throws a whole new game into the equation. People forced to attend often do not want to stop using and therefore change the dynamics for those that do. Along with the new accountability assessment and outcomes we started to have courts ordering clients to services. Prior to this change it was quite rare for a drug worker to push for the judge to give alternative to custody. I became quite skilled at requesting this decision of a judge; and because they didn't hear it often they agreed. But when it was applied as a way for all it changed the whole system to having rehabs with many people in them not wanting really to be clean but to avoid custody. This often puts clients who want to stay clean in a compromised position as they do not want to grass on their fellow clients, but the 'knowing' that another client has used can create cravings for them and they may wish to get it, so it makes it hard to be in a rehab and stay clean.

The outcome and assessment requirement further annoyed me as there is/was no standardised questionnaire to assess clients, with each services they were required to create their own, this was required by the funders; the health authorities. This is an interesting point cos normally within the health sector they have standardised assessments and outcome questionnaires used throughout the country developed through experience.

Services therefore had to create/provide these questionnaires which really were a waste of time, because the data couldn't be compared with any other service as everyone was designing them in isolation. And worse than that, crack users are often paranoid about answering any question on personal info, especially on their first visit to services. If I was to carry out the questionnaire not only would it have caused the paranoia to obstruct success but also my/their time is then taken up filling out pointless forms , and they may often not get the time to actually talk about the problem they have attended for. Therefore reducing self referral further. Consequently changing the structures of services to that similar to U.S.A and that was not compatible with my style that I had proven works.

Chapter 3 I outgrew my pot, and 'needed' pruned

Tapping

Back in 1995 I was paired up by my boss with an experienced trainer, who specialised in training staff on issues of racism. Together we developed the structure of the training around working with women crack users. We did it and it was very successful but we didn't get paid. My boss claimed after all money made was accounted for, only expenses were left for us. Oh is it, that's the last time I was going to do training for the service, making them money but disrespecting myself. In addition there was a Black organisation for Black drug workers, for which she was chair of and from my view she was squashed out of position by him. When she and I spoke on the phone, my education in phone tapping begun. We became good friends after the training and talked a lot on the phone. A clicking noise occurred, not always, not noticeable to me at first, but she pointed it out, 'what's that clicking? Your phones tapped'. We jokingly guessed words that caused the click for it seemed to respond to words. This never happened with anyone else I spoke to. I ignored it really, asked around about it, I knew I wasn't doing anything wrong so it didn't bother me, although intrigued to find out who's behind it.

A woman who was married to a politician told me of course 'they' will tap you, you have a high profile and they would just watch me for that reason. Also because the service had a very Black focus was another reason to watch me.

I also used to talk to my partner often on the phone and one day yes it clicked there. She heard it and had always told me be careful, you sure your boss ain't tapping you? Erm no I would say, and if so, well I only speaking truth.

Remember no payment for training. I had been developing services for Women crack cocaine users for 5 years, very successfully but I really wanted to help all areas that have contact with my client group.

My boss had me sit down in his office and on his white board he outlined the structure of how I could run training for social services, if I agreed he could bid social services for monies to employ me full time, I only worked 3 days a week. I agreed. Never was a full time post but I trained each team in the borough on how to work with women crack users. Nice.

I wanted to train staff in prisons and set up groups for women users. He said write it up, I did; it never transpired.
Months later another service was in the prisons, Holloway. They advertised posts, there were grass roots posts, which I would of liked but a manager would be placed above me, I didn't want that job, I wanted to train the staff and inmates to teach each other by imparting my knowledge but no. I wrote offering that package to them and was told that there wasn't really that many crack users in the prison yet, they would come to me if they needed me, but they never have. At that time my clients estimated for me that 60% of inmates were crack related clients.

I was frustrated that I couldn't spread out my knowledge and skills, it so empowered those I trained. Oh I thought I will do outreach, working women were getting notable in the area. It was a new area to me so I approached the few services that offered outreach but try as I did to go along with their staff to witness their approach it never transpired.
I had a woman I met whilst speaking at a conference in Birmingham March that year. She invited me down to see her

team and she was doing outreach, in Leicester I went with her and enjoyed it, she said there was a post coming up I said I wanted it, for I was feeling frustrated where I was working and sickened when my female clients would turn up and be looked at like a piece of dirt, by the male volunteers for the service. I did complain, but it was a man's world. One asked me if he could interview one of my female clients, I said No, she was vulnerable, next thing I knew, she is telling me he has asked her and she agreed, but didn't want to. I wasn't happy. I confronted him, he shrugged it off. I complained to my boss. He said put it in writing, I did and nothing happened. I asked why and my boss said 'oh if it is an official complaint you need to write that on it. So I did. A meeting was due to be held. Prior to this the harassing male volunteer wrote his response and all I know is he didn't appear very well educated and articulate when I had spoken to him, but on reading his response to my statement he wrote so eloquently , it was surprising he couldn't get a job, just like my boss.

I needed childcare in the building and highlighted it as an issue for years. I had a volunteer whom was extremely natural to the job, she had pre-school children but no child care, she was so determined to help in this field that she would bring them in with her. This was not ideal, we had nowhere for them to rest, play. I complained to my boss, how can I train women, when there is no child care. He said find somewhere tell him the cost and he will pay. And Pigs flew, she found a service I think it was £15 a day in total for both, they were twins. We told him, he said it was too much. We turned and left the room. No I was frustrated in my job and the health authorities were asking for assessments and outcomes, for no real good reason, only time consuming and stopping many who attempt to enter into services.

No it was time to leave , I complained to my boss and told him , you think I won't leave my clients ; and yes that was true, but when I find a way I will go.

Chapter 4 constructive dismisal

The tapping continued, same ol, same ol.

When I went to Leicester to look at outreach although nothing transpired regarding the post I found it led me to the answer, for the post was only part time and therefore in my creative self I come up with an idea I could do training for them to make them the money for my full time post, but twisted the concept a bit and came up with a solution, sell my training myself, create my own project and work with clients for free, all I needed was a place to meet them. My friend ran a community centre and had in past said if she could help in anyway she would. I asked her for use of the centre, she said yes. I could use all the facilities too, Brilliant.

Only problem was I knew nothing of how to pay tax, self employment rules. I found a government sponsored training available by the DTI - it was free and helped people setting up business. I attended it but didn't tell anyone at work my plans, just booked a few days off. The administrators' behaved peculiar asking where I was going when I book the few days leave; I said I was sorting things out at home.
I trained crack users in weights but this also included staff, the administrators no less, and after attending the course, they behaved quite cold towards me and didn't come to weight training anymore. Did they know something? On the back of the course we were also given a business advisor, whom helped us put our business plan together. This we needed to get start up business monies from the bank. I waited a response, 1997 came I was planning to resign at the end of the financial year. In all the years I had worked for the project I

had been employed 3 days a week, other than when I was setting up the weight training at the end of 1996, but around the same time as the bank loan request my boss asked that I could write up policies for women for the service, and outreach policies too. He said I could have a day a week to put it together, now all 5 days of the week would be taken. He asked how long I needed. 12 weeks I said. That went up to the end of the financial year. He seemed surprised, asking am I sure I could do it that fast. Yes I could and I did. But I didn't want all my free time tied up, or I would not be able to plan my business. So I said I would no longer be taking the weight training sessions and suggested they had someone else train to do it.

The bank refused the loan. Oh dear, what to do?
But remember the woman earlier married to a politician , well I thought she was a sister, but no, I told her of my plans for a better chance for women and she didn't want me to go so she told my boss, I think but truly I don't know. For he seemed to already know; as I felt it was consequential that I was writing up women's policies and outreach policies.

Anyway he called me in his office, along with my recently made supervisor/manager, whom was a bigot, and ignorant and had issues with me and my 'spoilt ' way. And here he said, chat had been going around that I was leaving, was it true? Was I leaving? No I replied, for I wasn't leaving as the bank had refused. After the meeting he told my manager /supervisor to get rid of me anyway she wanted. (I learnt this at a later date she told a college of mine with glee), so she started booking heroin clients into my diary, blocking my space so there would be no freedom to adapt to the instant gratification required by many crack users. I told her please do not put anymore in for me, but she continued. In the end I refused to do anymore. I received a letter from her saying this was my written warning and I will follow instructions and a hearing would be held. I had previously joined a union, much to their surprise when I introduced my rep into the equation. I was being constructively dismissed but should I waste my time fighting them, they didn't want me, I didn't want to be there; in that atmosphere anyway. The Black male youths whom when first started training loved me, yet after they became Muslim they didn't like me anymore. Word got to my ears that they saw me as a cracker, a white slave handler, and a lesbian too. One even said he couldn't be seen talking to me.

No the best thing to do would be to leave, jump ship, sink or swim. I booked the rest of my owed holiday for the end of the month, after the date of my disciplinary hearing.
On the day of the hearing everyone listen and then washed over their heads, was my words of truth, I hadn't done anything wrong, but my supervisor had behaved unfairly. They asked how many clients I had, this was hard to count; with crack users for they often don't attend regularly, so I said 21, which was the number of hours I was employed for, but in truth I counted 45, for I counted how many visiting clients I had had in the last 3 months, so they were still my clients on paper. They said yes they could see I don't need anymore but obviously my supervisor had misunderstood how I ran my service and so they recommended I write how my crack service ran. She said comfortingly smug 'is that ok Louise?', 'oh yes 'I said. I left the room and placed my previously typed resignation in her pigeon hole along with my bosses, whom was sitting across the room as I did so. I had a couple of weeks left to serve there and then into the world of the unknown.

Chapter 5   I found a way ; free at last

I had made good relations with a community centre in the area over my years of working in the drug service, and they had previously told me they would be willing to help me regarding women crack users anyway they could. I therefore approached the centre and asked that I could use their facilities to counsel my clients for free. They agreed for me to use their facilities free of charge and therefore I create my own independent service to run from there; which was actually a better venue for women to attend as they can remain anonymous, as to why they are coming to the building.

I put together a training package and mailed it to appropriate services,. Although I made a lot of effort to sell the training to services only a few took it up but Those that did benefited greatly as a team, but even though I wanted to train teams, it seemed services preferred to train one member of staff and then they could come back and train the team, at that time. I took all my crack using clients with me to the community centre and started doing agency care work to supplement my income.

Throughout my adult life I had had back problems, not bad, but every few years, I was unable to walk, get up for a few days, usually when I was stressed in life. My back started giving me pain and where I would have always rested to recover , I didn't I took pain killers , so I could go to work, no sick pay in agency work. My back got progressively worse until one day I was in agony (march 1998) , couldn't get up , couldn't move , couldn't get relief from the pain. I called out a doctor , she phoned the hospital , they said I should have volterol , I could only have one every 12 hours , thus if I needed any before then to call for an ambulance , by evening I was in agony again. So I called the ambulance and was taken to hospital. 13 hours later I got a bed. X rays showed nothing other than I had arthritis in my spine; which fascinated surgeons as I was only 37. Eventually I had a MIR scan, which showed I had a prolapsed disc ; they said surgery I said no I would heal myself. This was all a bit of a shock at the time for I was healthy, did weight training, dancing, lived well yet they wanted to do surgery on my spine. They injected it but that didn't help. They then plastered my body and I was sent home with crutches.

Just weeks prior to this I was approached by 'Community care ' magazine journalist, Audrey Thompson She had the task of asking services what they thought of the Governments new outcomes and assessment policy. But due to services fearing they may have funding removed they refused to speak out against the policy. Would I? Of course I wasn't asking for their funding anyway. And had set up on my own because I felt it was the only way. In her article I explained what was wrong with the policy and then other people in the drugs field said how wrong I was. The published article came out whilst I lay in hospital, so my timing was spot on. There was a lovely photo of me in the article where I am holding myself up on work surface, no sign I am in so much pain.

 I tried everything I had pain killers but also went to a Chinese doctor for herbs, acupuncture and massage. I read Susan Hayes, worked through as much emotional baggage I could find, loads of lateral thinking. Whilst in plaster I could lay on my back , but after a few weeks it was removed and then I could only lay on my front or side , most of the time I had a guy come and do reflexology make me hold some bar things that supposedly destroyed free radicals and he cooked me Ital food. I was well looked after during this time.

But what about the phone tapping you may ask. Yes it continued on after me leaving my job and developed a new trick, the phone would squeak at night like a mouse (a bit of a ring tone). I phoned BT and said my phone was tapped could they sort it. The guy just ridiculed me, saying 'why would your phone be tapped?' I told him about the squeaking and he said 'oh that's where they are testing the line; I said every night!? . He said yes. I could see that was a waste of time. But on my spine collapsing the squeaking stopped.

I spent 9 months trying to heal myself, got a little shuffle going, could walk slowly for 20 minutes, then bam! I was back down again in agony. I decided to have the surgery. Which I did on the 4Th November 1998. A significant date you will see. It went perfect and I was home after 4 days, and the squeak returned to the phone instantly, to welcome me straight away.

Along with the phone intimidation came another variable. Prior to my spine problem when I opened my new service a car would park outside my building with its engine running all evening ;with their lights on, with 2 white guys , looked a bit like police but I don't think they were.

I slowly become stronger again and returned to my community centre and out reached to gather clients again. I had done enough thinking lying there for 9 months and decided to try and hire venues and sell individual seats for training .It worked I was selling out every event. The training lasted 7 hours so it was a strain on my back but I just included rest into my schedule after training and only did one day a month. It worked I trained all over the country as well as

Scotland and Ireland. Everything was going smoothly then..........

To read more on my journey go to my web site –

www.higherinsight.webs.com

A poem I was inspired to write 95

Basing Racing

Manic men a chasing

can't find a way out

gonna be wipe out

Why see the window

when all lights say go!

Now going solo

trying to make

dough

Haven't sat down

as of yet

what was yesterday?

Oh I forget

Can't see tomorrow

on a rapid mind flow

can't seem to let go

lay my head

but still No!

Hearts a drumming solo

Heads a fuzzing

fuse blow

Body tense alivo

Ready steady

set go!

Time to pull on up

charge my engine up

rest a little

cool it down

replace harmony

in this town

Deeper breathing

Mind a clearing

Reality is now

appearing

Stop using Crack/Cocaine and reclaim your life.

Must avoid
known suffering
If this life
I am to win

Maintain my health
in mind body
and soul
stay contented
in a complete
whole

Work to get
what I knows
right
so I can come
to meet the night

New awakening
has occurred
feels so strange
and obscured
facing my reality

recognising
what's not me

Finding what is whom
I am
Feeling I will lose
the plan

so unfamiliar
with this view
Yet ok old
present and new

Where I'm going
I'm not sure
I have opened
a huge door

I need to learn
the world it brings
recognising
the change in things

Reality faced

head on

so near I need to see

and gone

I'm doing fine

but should learn caution

I only have

a small portion

fearlessly treading

then observing the point

which brings awareness

of the hint

To back off that danger

I need to see

I need to have

reality

To boldly go

where others fear to tread

I hope to learn

to think ahead

To see the danger

before it's done

I hope I soon

will overcome

No thank you crack man (1995)

The crack man in your head
will kill you dead

in the brain cell
in the life style
in the K-os
and it will cost

cost your mind
cost your body
cost your soul

You will give all
to retain all
But you will fall
a victim
to that man

He offers great gifts
and a mind lift
from the day shift

your involved

but he cannot bring
more than suffering
from the craving
You'll endure

Let the crack man
give not one gram
of his seductive ways
to capture you

For his patient ways
will take as many days
to worm all his way
to your minds view

It just depends on you
to allow him through
down an avenue
to no revenue[i]

So take no chance

give not one glance

to the crack man

on your door

It is no life

to be a pipes wife

with a lift that has no floor

So come on take a look

at what else could hook

your energy

you posses

Use your daring courage

for some lifetime voyage

to the destiny

you dare to wish

Give your self a chance

see how you advance

to your completion's

of your goals

have a nice one

in your life to come

make your destiny

a fulfilling one

It's your life

Make the right choice!!!!!!

Stop using Crack/Cocaine and reclaim your life.

Printed in Great Britain
by Amazon